Make It Your
Ambition

Published by

370 S. Lowe Ave., Ste. A
PMB 211
Cookeville, TN 38501
1-800-211-8793
books@notgrass.com
www.notgrass.com

ISBN 1-933410-26-4 (paperback)
Printed in the United States of America

Portions of this book originally appeared as articles in *Home School Digest*, the Christian Family Discipleship Quarterly for serious homeschoolers. Each issue nearly 100 pages! Subscriptions: $18/year. Contact: Wisdom's Gate, P.O. Box 374, Covert, MI 49043. Phone: 800-343-1943. www.homeschooldigest.com Used by permission. All rights reserved.

Dedicated to my parents,
Ray and Charlene Notgrass,
who taught me to seek the Lord,
and to the wife I look forward to knowing
at the proper time.

Special Thanks

My friends at Wisdom's Gate have given me a forum in the *Home School Digest* to develop and communicate many of these ideas. I thank Skeet, Sony, Israel, Grace, Mercy, Bethany, and Glory for their encouragement.

Several friends kindly previewed my book and provided me with feedback that helped make it better — Irene Anderson, Jim Angle, Tammie Brown, Clint Diggs, Duane Dixon, Jim Bob Duggar, Jon Glick, R.J. and Elaine Moore, Cody Moore, Sandi Queen, Larry and Laura Raper, Lance and Debi Reynolds, Charlie Spiller, Camden Spiller, and Riley Spiller. Kiley Queen especially searched for grammatical and spelling errors. Thank you!

My father Ray, mother Charlene, and sisters Bethany and Mary Evelyn helped get the book ready to print and helped me make time to write it in the first place. My family members have been supporting my efforts for 26 years, and I thank Dad, Mom, Bethany, Mary Evelyn, Liz, Hannah, Daniel, and Granddaddy Wes for enjoying life with me.

John Notgrass
Gainesboro, TN
March 23, 2005

Contents

Make It Your Ambition.................................7

Dream Big...13

Is God's Will Missing?.............................23

Lessons From Joshua...............................29

Honor Your Father and Mother....................37

Why I Plan to Train My Children at Home.........47

Home Education Past High School................51

So You Want to Be a Millionaire?................61

Being Different...................................77

What God Joins Together.........................83

Receiving Children for God's Glory..............113

Civic Duties.....................................123

The Household of God............................133

Make it your ambition to lead a quiet life,
to mind your own business,
and to work with your own hands,
as we commanded you;
so that you may conduct yourself decently
toward outsiders, and have need of nothing.

1 Thessalonians 4:11-12

Chapter 1

Make It Your Ambition

You have tremendous opportunities ahead of you. Take advantage of them. Do not let people despise your youth because you fail to use well this time in your life. Set an example for the people around you by your words and deeds. Keep growing in the grace and knowledge of our Lord Jesus Christ. Make it your ambition to be a devoted disciple.

Like everyone else on earth, you must decide whom you are going to serve with your life. You can go along with the crowd, fritter your life away in empty pursuits, and lose everything worth having in the end. Or you can follow the sometimes lonely path toward heaven, invest your life in God's service, and gain everything worth having in the end. When we stop to consider this simple comparison, the choice is not much of a choice. Only the second option will satisfy our deepest longings.

A Great Trust

Our parents have trained us from birth. They have given us knowledge and skills and taught us first of all to fear the Lord. We should be thankful for the lessons they have learned the hard way, for the sacrifices they have made for our benefit, and for the opportunities they have enabled us to enjoy.

We have spent so many years being different from our peers, and we have developed such a different view of life, that we do not want to follow the example of our peers. Many of them are going to college, getting a degree they will not use, getting married, working a 9-to-5 job, having a couple of kids, and buying a suburban house with a mortgage. Later on they will have a mid-life crisis, retire, play golf, and die in a nursing home. I have different goals for my life.

I would like to marry and have children (more than two, God willing), but that desire is part of my long-term vision for serving the Lord. We who have come to know the Lord at the feet of godly parents have received a great trust. God has given us a head start on making a positive difference in our generation and on rearing another generation of godly children.

Since we want our children and our children's children to be faithful to the Lord, what should we do now to work toward that goal? For those of us who desire to marry, that is one of the primary questions we must address. Parents cannot force their children to follow the Lord, but parents are responsible for their failure to train their children properly (Jer. 5:7). How will our decisions now about work, finance, education, and other areas affect our parenting ability later?

Even if we are blessed with faithful parents, we do not have a free ride to success on earth and a home in heaven.

We must make the same decision that those who do not have faithful parents must make. That is, each of us must make a conscious, personal decision to walk in the good way. Our families affect us greatly for good or evil, but ultimately, each of us is responsible for his or her own actions (Eze. 18). As we grow older and earn the freedom to make more choices about how and where we spend our time, we must also accept the responsibility that comes with that freedom.

The Foundation

God's word tells us how to use the liberty we have in Christ. The Bible is the foundation on which we must build healthy families, churches, and communities. We cannot ignore the beauty and power of its instruction if we wish truly to succeed.

Scripture is sufficient and efficient to prepare us to live as God desires. Our world has all sorts of experts who provide special counsel to others. Sadly, many of them offer their own brand of what is falsely called knowledge (1 Tim. 6:20), and none of them can match the true wisdom which God has revealed to us. We should examine for ourselves what Scripture says and learn to discern good teaching from bad.

Our culture has as many idols as any ancient civilization. We may use different names and give them different shapes, but still we have the temptation to give our attention to created things rather than to the Creator. Wealth, security, popularity, entertainment, and more vie for our time and focus. Worry and frustration necessarily accompany any effort to make it on one's own. Self-gratification is not all it is cracked up to be. It leaves its victims cold and lonely.

When I am thinking clearly, I easily confess that God is in control and that everything will work out for good under his direction. However, when I allow the minimal pressures of my young life to cloud my vision, I start worrying about how everything will turn out. Seeking first God's kingdom and righteousness puts everything else in perspective. We must keep our eyes fixed on Jesus and press on toward the goal. We must trust the Lord with all of our hearts and acknowledge him in all of our ways.

Ignorance of God's word leaves us undefended against spiritual attacks. Many of our peers do not know basic facts about Bible people and events, much less the deeper concepts of Scripture. They may claim to know Biblical principles, but that is not the same as knowing the Bible. "I think" is not the same as "God says."

Our knowledge and understanding of God's word should continually grow. We do not live on earth long enough to exhaust its deep mines of wisdom. We should not stake our claim on the teachings of any one man or denomination and then assume that we have all the answers. Other believers, past and present, can help us to see things that we have missed. Together we can build up Christ's church in our generation.

We may not share messages before large audiences, but all of us know people whom we can encourage and exhort in God's way. Neither personal pride nor self-righteousness should motivate us in this sharing of God's truth. We are not spiritual aristocrats condescending to help the lowly. As someone has said, we are spiritual beggars helping other beggars find bread.

Youthfulness does not disqualify us or exempt us from teaching others. God can use infants to prepare praise, and he can use young men and women to communicate his message. Young people who know the Lord have more to share than old people with a wall full of credentials and a heart empty of faith. Be humble. Be confident. Bless other people with God's truth.

Reflections

The following chapters provide my observations on several issues of significance. My burden is especially for other young men. Some young men I know have been drifting through their 20s without direction. Their training in public school and college has left them unprepared for real life. They have poor vision for where they want to go in life, so they are struggling to get ahead in the true spiritual sense.

Perhaps I can help you avoid some of the pain and struggle I have seen others face and have experienced myself. God cares about our family life, our education, our work, our money management, and our social interaction. He cares so much that he has told us how we can honor him in these areas.

Based on my study and experience, these are things that I am trying to put into practice in my life. I do not want to be like the Pharisees, chaining others down with burdens that I am unwilling to lift myself. I have not already attained completion in these areas. I must continue the daily struggle with my flesh to subdue my selfish desires, lest I, having preached these things to others, should myself become a castaway (1 Cor. 9:27).

I expect my understanding of these issues to deepen in coming years, but I also expect my core principles to remain the same. Please do not accept my perspective as your final authority. Explore these ideas for yourself and discuss them with your parents and other wise people around you. I do not expect you to do everything the same way I do, but I do expect you to think about the issues, make conscious decisions, and live them out confidently.

Of the few Greek words I know, one of my favorites is *parakaleo* (par-ah-kal-eh'-o). As used in Titus 2:6, for example, it literally means "to call alongside," that is, to encourage or to exhort. I am calling you alongside to share ideas with you, to encourage you in your efforts, and to exhort you to press on toward maturity.

My prayer is that these words will challenge and encourage you to appreciate the blessings of home, to dream big dreams, and to pursue a life of holiness. We need to take advantage of our current opportunities and prepare well for our future roles. We need to fulfill our purpose in our generation. To know and serve the Lord is the highest possible ambition, the only purpose to which we should devote our lives.

Chapter 2

Dream Big

Where are you headed with your life? Do you have a vision, a long-term goal? Have you thought about the influence of your life on future generations? Or are you focused on yourself and what you want now?

You could pursue many things. Like the builders at Babel, you could seek to make a name for yourself on earth (Gen. 11:4). Like David's son Absalom, you could chase power, letting no one, not even your father, stand in your way (2 Sam. 15-18). You could love the wages of unrighteousness like Balaam and wear yourself out getting rich (2 Pet. 2:15). Or like Zimri you could satisfy your passion to your own shame and ruin (Num. 25). All of these pursuits have appeal, but their thrills are temporary. Since they do not meet your deepest needs, they will leave you empty in the end.

The best the world has to offer pales in comparison with what God has to offer. We must set our minds on things above, looking beyond the me, the here, and the now. We should seek a glimpse of the big picture to find our place in God's great scheme of things.

My parents have been successful parents because they have passed on to me this central vision:

We pray and work that we, our children, our grandchildren, and all of our descendants will be faithful to Jesus Christ forever.

That is a big dream. We cannot aim for anything higher than that in our family, for nothing is more important than spiritual unity with God. We cannot aim for anything less either, for we could not be satisfied with unfaithfulness.

The Rechabites wonderfully illustrated the possibility and power of long-term faithfulness (Jer. 35). God expects faithfulness in me and in those who come after me, and I do not want to disappoint him. As long as this earth endures, I want my descendants to know and cling to their first love, Jesus Christ. I want Christ to find faith in my family (Luke 18:8).

I want all people, believers and unbelievers, to look at my family and give glory to God. When they see my relationship with my wife, I want them to see something of Christ's relationship with the church, his bride. When they see my relationship with my children, I want them to see something of God's love for his children. When they look at my family, I want them to understand better what life is about. I want my family to be a living parable, thrown alongside the good news of Jesus Christ, and used by God to accomplish his will.

God has saved me and called me to a holy life, not because of anything I have done, but because of his own purpose and grace. I died, and my life is now hidden with Christ in God. Whatever I do, whether in word or deed, I want to do all in the name of the Lord Jesus, giving thanks to God the Father through him. Even though I do not know exactly where he will lead me on earth, I know that my times are in his hands.

I am an alien and a stranger in this world. I must abstain from the sinful desires that wage war against my soul. I want to live such a good life among the pagans that, even if they accuse me of doing wrong, they will see my good deeds and glorify God on the day he visits us.

Being Content

As we wonder about what God might do with our lives in the future, we must remember to be content with our current situation. Paul said that he had learned to be content in all circumstances (Phil. 4:11). He was not talking about having spinach for supper or having to get up early to milk the goats. Paul faced hunger and suffered need. In addition he was beaten and stoned and shipwrecked and imprisoned and cold. I have had an easy life compared to his!

Why do I have trouble being content? Discontent is a manifestation of ingratitude, which rears its head in my life. As I dream big dreams about what I might accomplish for God, I get frustrated when things do not move as fast as I would like. That is my problem. I am focused on what I want rather than what God knows is best.

One of the desires of my heart is to marry a woman of God and to rear children for God's glory, but the fulfillment of that desire is still in the unknown future. Why must I keep waiting? Have my parents not trained me to be a good husband and father? Does God not want me to serve him in that way? Why must I hear about weddings of people who are not ready for marriage (in my opinion) while I am still a bachelor? Even if I am mature enough for marriage, how will I ever afford to build and prepare a home for my wife and children?

If I am not content as an unmarried man, why should I expect to be content as a married man? Marriage is a blessed arrangement, but it brings its own set of challenges, too. Maybe I will not marry. Maybe God wants to use me in another way. If that is what he wants, who am I to grumble for something else? Even if I do marry in the future, I am apparently not ready now. Joseph was 30 when he married, Isaac was 40, and Jacob was apparently pushing 75, so I should not feel too bad!

Right now I can enjoy sharing a room with my little brother. I can enjoy spending time with my sisters. I can enjoy growing with my parents. I can enjoy all of the familiar traditions and experiences that have kept our family going for the past two and a half decades.

As my grandfather needs extra attention, I am also able to help my father care for him. That special assignment has encouraged me to be more patient. We do not know how much longer Granddaddy will be with us, so I need to take advantage of this opportunity for service.

I expect the girl I marry to wait patiently for me and to prepare herself to be my helper. I need to prepare patiently to be her protector and provider, and when the times comes, to seek her hand. Then we can begin shaping our own set of family traditions and experiences, and we can build a household of faith that continues the heritage of our parents.

When I compare myself to others, I may think that I am getting short changed. When, however, I think about how much I already have, I see how foolish I am. I have a godly father and mother who have trained me in God's way. I have five siblings and a grandfather with whom to share everyday life. I have plenty to eat, plenty to wear, and a comfortable house. I am part of an encouraging congregation of saints that helps me live for God. The list goes on and on. Above all the earthly blessings, I am even blessed with all spiritual blessings in Christ.

We humans like to compare ourselves with each other. Often we are jealous of people who are richer, prettier, funnier, or stronger. Often we are condescending toward those who are poorer, uglier, nerdier, or weaker. I know I would be better off if I stopped comparing myself with others. That is what usually leads to my discontent — comparing myself with others.

Sometimes I wonder what my life would be like if I lived in a different place or time, had different resources at my disposal, or grew up with different training. All such thoughts are ridiculous if I am trying to figure out how my life could have been better. God raised me up as he saw fit, equipped me as he saw fit, and put me in this place and time to accomplish his purpose in my generation (Acts 13:36). I am alive, here and now, for a good reason. I should make the most of it.

If discontent shows ingratitude, then contentment shows thankfulness. Instead of wondering how my life could be better, I should seek to learn how I can make life better for others. How would my family be better if I had not spoken that unkind word? How would the widow's life be better if I had stopped by to see her last week? How much more could I accomplish if I managed my time more effectively?

Being content is not dependent on our circumstances, our feelings, or our desires. We cannot wait to be content until it is easy. Instead of asking, "Why, God, do you treat me like this after all I have done for you?", we should ask, "Why, God, do I treat you like this after all you have done for me?"

Being Good

I came to Jesus with a big debt of sin. I was deep in the hole from the start. He paid the price for me, and my good works cannot balance the scales. I cannot be careless about how I live, however. Careless living is a slap in the face of Christ. If I am truly thankful for how God has blessed me, then I will show it by my attitude and actions.

I have to be careful about what I say. I have to be careful about what I think. I have to be careful about how I interact with other people. I have to be careful about how I spend my time and my money. I have to be careful about how I dress, how I drive, how I work, and how I play. I have to be careful about what I watch, what I hear, and what I read. I even have to be careful about how I eat and sleep so I can keep my body in good condition.

Whew! Do I have to take everything so seriously? Can I ever let my guard down and get away with a little something? Do I have to be good all the time? Yes, I have to be good all the time, because I am not my own. I am living on borrowed time with borrowed possessions in a borrowed body. Even if we faithfully follow every commandment and make the most of every opportunity, we are only unworthy slaves doing what we ought to do (Luke 17:10).

I ought to be good all of the time, but I am not. Being good just some of the time is hard enough, and I struggle to do even that. I have to discipline myself. I have to put aside my selfish desires. I have to look out for other people.

Being bad draws the attention of the newspapers and TV shows. Being good often goes unnoticed. Sometimes we are even snubbed or criticized for trying to do right. Regardless of what other people think, however, pursuing holiness shows that we are thankful for how God has blessed us.

I'll See It When I Believe It

Do you identify with the father who cried out to Jesus, "I believe. Help my unbelief!" (Mark 9:24)? I do. Jesus said that all things are possible to him who believes, yet I fail to take him at his word. When challenged to consider spiritual truth, the skeptic scoffs, "I'll believe it when I see it." The disciple, when thus challenged, should respond with humility, "I'll see it when I believe it."

When we believe, then we can see what God has in store for us. Believing is much more than mental assent. Believing means living out the implications of what we acknowledge in our minds. In other words, faith without works is dead.

Enoch could not wait to start walking with God until he saw his reward. He had to believe that God rewards those who seek him and then live by that belief. Noah could not wait until the rain started to begin building the ark. He had to take God's message seriously and act upon it. Abraham did not have a map and a travel guide when God told him to leave his country and kindred. He had to start moving, not even knowing where he was going.

These and other examples from the letter to the Hebrews illustrate for us what happens when God's people believe: they conquer kingdoms, they effect righteousness, they shut the mouths of lions, they quench the power of fire, they bear up under torture. All things are possible to him who believes.

The petty things that I worry about pale in comparison with the challenges faced by faithful men and women of old. I should not struggle to "keep my hopes up" when faith is the substance of things hoped for. The simple answer for every doubt I have about work, money, education, and marriage is "I'll see it when I believe it." God will provide when I trust that he is able. He may not provide what I think I want when I think I want it; but if he does not, then he will provide something better at a better time.

Again, believing and doing go together. If I said that God could provide my daily bread but refused to work diligently, then I would be a lazy fool. If I wore myself out to get riches and did not acknowledge God as the source of all blessings, then I would be a busy fool. If I refused to recognize God's provision and loafed around, then I would be a plain old fool. The only wise alternative is to trust that God will provide and to act upon his instructions. I'll see it when I believe it.

We have not seen heaven. We have read about it, and we have testimony from someone who has been there (Jesus). Still we have not seen it. Some accuse us of waiting for pie in the sky by and by, but they do not understand faith. We cannot wait to believe until the end comes and we realize what we have ignored.

We must believe now, when we are surrounded by doubters. We must believe now, when we see dimly and know partially. If we can trust the Lord for eternity, then we can surely trust the Lord for today. Yet that is the struggle that you and I face — to trust the Lord for today.

Are you waiting to believe it when you see it, or are you willing to see it when you believe it? All things are possible to him who believes. Count on it.

Building for the Future

Hezekiah was a good king of Judah. He restored the temple, destroyed the idols, and started leading the people back into obedience to God. The people honored him when he died. However, Hezekiah apparently suffered from limited vision for the future.

Hezekiah knew that his descendents and his nation were soon going to face captivity in Babylon, but he was content that he had peace and truth during his reign (2 Kin. 20:19). His son Manasseh became king at age 12, and he did evil in the sight of the Lord. Manasseh brought idolatry back into prominence. He indulged in witchcraft and spiritualism. He even put an idol in the temple.

The Lord spoke to Manasseh and the people, but Manasseh would not pay attention until he was taken as a prisoner to Babylon. There in his distress he finally humbled himself and recognized the God of his fathers. God brought him back to finish his lengthy reign, and Manasseh tried to undo much of the harm he had caused.

Manasseh's son Amon, however, had a wicked two year reign before he was assassinated. Hezekiah's great-grandson Josiah came to the throne at age eight and reigned well for 31 years. He had to undo the work of his father and grandfather. Josiah died in battle against the Egyptians, and the Jews were soon taken into Babylonian captivity.

Hezekiah, like all of us, struggled with a mixture of good and bad motives. I am not so naive as to believe that we can create a perfect community of faith on earth simply by following a specific set of rules. However, though we are imperfect, we cannot be satisfied with unfaithfulness. We must consecrate ourselves to the Lord, ridding ourselves of unclean practices.

As we offer praise and thanksgiving to God, we must continually search the Scriptures to understand the good and right way we should take. We must accept God's forgiveness of our sins and go on joyfully in obedience. We must destroy the idols that block our view. We must trust firmly, give generously, and endure patiently the struggles we face as God's disciples.

We must commit ourselves to restoring God's ways in all areas of life. We must keep our eyes fixed on Jesus, the author and perfecter of our faith. We must be content with what we have and where we are, even as we anticipate better things in the future. We must pursue holiness, without which we cannot see the Lord.

If we focus only on ourselves, then future generations will be unprepared to take up the banner of faith. Let us develop and maintain a long-term vision of faithfulness so that generations to come will know and serve the King of Kings.

What Matters in the End

At the end of your life, what will be more important to you: How many awards you won or how many friends you made? How much treasure you saved in a retirement account or how much treasure you stored in heaven? How much you got out of life or how much you gave?

When your children and grandchildren and other people you influenced think about your life, what will stand out in their minds? Will they regret the way you squandered your time and talents? Or will they remember you as a faithful man or woman of God?

Stretch. Grow. Expand. Be bold and daring. Do not wait for good things to happen to you. Make good things happen for others. With God all things are possible.

Dream big.

Chapter 3

Is God's Will Missing?

Imagine a modern believer seeking the answer to a puzzling question about what he ought to do in a specific situation. He wants to do what is right, so he prays, asks for signs, and in other ways attempts to discern "God's will for his life."

He knows that the Bible is a rich source of wisdom, but he does not want to invest the time necessary to find the answer to this question. Simply looking up a few references in a concordance will not provide the broader context he needs to understand them. Maybe he is even afraid of the answer he will find in the Bible. He would prefer a personal word from the Lord to direct his steps.

This practice has bothered me for some time. First, it does not seem to work for me. Am I jealous? Am I too blind or too proud to acknowledge the efficacy of this process? Am I lacking in spiritual maturity? Second, I am not sure that this practice is correct. Should we expect God to give us specific, personal instruction about issues we face so that we can be inside his will?

What Is God's Will?

The Bible speaks of God's eternal determined will, the things that God wanted and therefore brought to pass. The prime example of this expression of God's will is the Lamb who was foreknown before the foundation of the world (1 Pet. 1:20). Jesus was delivered up by the predetermined plan and foreknowledge of God (Acts 2:23). God's hand and purpose predestined the actions taken by Herod, Pilate, the Gentiles, and the Jews who put Jesus to death (Acts 4:27-28). The Son of Man went as it had been determined (Luke 22:42). The Messiah had to suffer and be glorified (Luke 24:25, cf. Isa. 52:13-53:12). Jesus asked the Father to remove this cup from him, but Jesus submitted his will to the Father's will (Luke 22:42, Gal. 1:4).

God works in the world through natural and supernatural means to accomplish his purposes. He knows me. He knows my heart. He knows the number of hairs on my head. I believe that he knows whom I will marry, how many children I will have, what works I will accomplish on earth, and when I will die. This belief gives me comfort. However, I do not expect God to give me miraculous instructions about these things. He can do so; and if he does, then that will be fine with me. If he does not, then I must make plans and decisions based on the wisdom revealed in the Bible. Those plans will turn out as the Lord wills.

The Bible also speaks of God's desired moral will, which it connects with God's law. The idea in Psalm 40:8 (partially quoted in relation to Jesus in Hebrews 10:7) compares delighting to do God's will with having his law in the heart. Ezra exhorted the Israelites to do God's will by separating from the foreign wives they had taken (Ezra 10:11). Luke describes the Pharisees and lawyers as having rejected God's purpose by not accepting John's baptism (Luke 7:30).

Jesus said that those who do God's will are his family members (Mark 3:35). Those who want to do God's will know whether the teaching of Christ is divine or not (John 7:17). We are to do the will of God from the heart (Eph. 6:6). Epaphras prayed that the Colossians would be perfect and complete in all God's will (Col. 4:12). Peter contrasts living according to fleshly lusts with living according to God's will (1 Pet. 4:2).

What is God's will? God's will is that we be sanctified, avoiding fornication (1 Thess. 4:3). God's will is that we give thanks in all things (1 Thess. 5:18). God's will is that we do what is right, silencing the ignorance of foolish men (1 Pet. 2:15). God's good, pleasing, and perfect will is what we are able to prove when we are transformed by the renewing of our minds (Rom. 12:2).

I recognize God's eternal determined will, which he exercises over his creation to accomplish his plan. I also recognize God's revealed moral will, which some people follow and some do not. Does the Bible describe a third "personal will" which God has for each individual, a specific plan that each person must figure out in order to be pleasing to God?

Seeking God's Will

The list of possible questions is endless, but here are a few possibilities. Should I serve my dinner guests beef or chicken? Should I buy a cheap computer device made in

China or a slightly more expensive one made in Taiwan? Should I go to Florida or Canada on vacation? Should I work as a doctor or a janitor?

Theoretically each of these questions has one and only one right answer. Practically, however, some questions have more than one acceptable answer. We make plans and decisions based on the information available to us.

Paul made plans during his journeys around the Mediterranean. Sometimes his plans worked out; sometimes they did not. As James instructed the believers (Jam. 4:15), so Paul conditioned the execution of his plans upon the will of God (Rom. 1:10, 15:32; 1 Cor. 4:19, 16:7). Sometimes God intervened to prevent him from going to a certain location (Acts 16:6-7), and sometimes God specifically called him to go somewhere else (Acts 16:9-10). Paul did not seem to wait for God to tell him what to do next, but he knew that regardless of the plans he made, God might have something else in mind.

In the past God called specific people to do specific tasks, even unusual tasks. For example, he instructed Isaiah to walk around like a prisoner of war, naked and barefoot for three years, as a sign against Egypt and Cush (Isa. 20). Even though Isaiah was likely not completely unclothed, this is not recommended as a general practice for God's people. Likewise, God told Ezekiel to bake bread over human dung and eat it as a sign to the Israelites. God allowed Ezekiel to substitute cow's dung, but still this was an unusual practice (Eze. 4:9-17). Hosea, another prophet, received God's instruction to take a wife of harlotry (Hos. 1:2).

These were evidently clear commands from God rather than ideas that the prophets thought up and asked the Lord for the go ahead to do. Unless we receive direct, unmistakable instruction from the Lord, we should not assume that God secretly wants us to do something that violates his revealed moral will. If we have the option to do something that does not violate God's revealed moral will, then we do not need a special revelation. We can make a decision based on the guidance God has already provided.

How We Know What to Do

I have two basic problems with the modern search for "God's personal will for my life." First, it is vague and indecisive. It is based on feelings and circumstances rather than on wisdom and clear instruction. When I make a good decision, I usually feel good about it, at least when I look back on it in the future. However, I might also feel good at the time I make a bad decision. I still struggle against my fleshly desires and human wisdom, so I cannot depend on my feelings as a reliable guide.

Second, seeking God's specific will for a specific situation is usually unnecessary for one of three reasons. 1) The situation under consideration has relatively unimportant consequences. 2) The situation has no good options available. 3) The situation presents one clearly good option.

1) Someone could seek God's will on a matter with relatively unimportant consequences. Should I have eggs or cereal for breakfast? Should I read G.A. Henty's *Wulf the Saxon* or *With Lee in Virginia* next? If, in order to please God, I must consciously choose to do everything exactly as he has planned, then even questions like these take on great importance.

2) Someone may seek God's will on a situation with no good options. Whom should I take on a date next Friday: Sally or Jane? The answer is neither, because pursuing temporary romantic relationships is wrong. Expecting to

receive a good answer from the Lord to a question with no good answers is a waste of time.

3) Someone may have a clear choice between one good and one bad option. Should I marry a believer or an unbeliever? Should I do simple work that allows family discipleship or take a high-paying job that hurts my family? Our decision-making process becomes blurry when we let emotions and selfish desires interfere with it, but many times the correct choice is obvious.

Not all questions stand out clearly to us in black and white. How should we respond when we face an issue that is a real dilemma? We should go to the Bible. Paul told Timothy that the God-breathed Scriptures are profitable for teaching, reproof, correction, and training in righteousness that the man of God may be thoroughly equipped for every good work (2 Tim. 3:16-17).

Do the Scriptures provide inadequate instruction for any decision we face in life? Can I decide how to spend my time and money based on the teaching of Scripture? Can I choose a good wife based on the teaching of Scripture? If we feel unprepared to make such decisions on our own, we can seek the counsel of those who have more experience with Scripture and pray to God for wisdom.

I fear that I often want God to give me specific, personal direction because I am not satisfied with the answers he has already given us in the Bible. Often I know what I ought to do, but I want God to let me be an exception. I want some kind of higher wisdom than what is available to everyone else.

God may give us special, personal assignments, but he has told us what he wants us to do in the meantime. Since we do not know what is going to happen tomorrow, we should make plans based on wisdom and let tomorrow worry about itself.

Chapter 4

Lessons From Joshua

The fifth chapter of Joshua describes a generation of God's people coming of age and preparing to do their duty. Does that sound familiar to you? Are you ready to take on the challenges of our generation?

This passage has several lessons that are of value to our study. It shows us that we should make a difference in the world, that men are usually responsible for problems, that following God's ways can be painful, that God wants to give us something better than we have now, and that we should be on God's side.

The history of the Old Testament is true. It is valuable as an historical record of God's dealings with man. It also offers us spiritual lessons through the good and bad examples of the characters we see. As Paul told us, the things written in the past were written to teach us (Rom. 15:5).

1) We should make a difference in the world.

The first verse of Joshua 5 tells how the pagan kings were afraid of the sons of Israel when they heard how the Lord had dried up the waters of the Jordan. Do worldly leaders fear us today? Do believers play such a prominent role in society that unbelievers are afraid of our influence?

I am not talking about physical intimidation in our case. I am talking about allowing God to work through us to make a difference in the world. God has used certain individuals and groups to make a valuable impact in recent years; but overall, the positive influence of the church seems to have decreased in the United States and other Western countries. We should expect family problems, substance abuse, vile entertainment, and other social ills when we fail to follow God's ways. Because the church has not effectively addressed these problems even among its own members, the influence of bad continues to grow while the influence of good declines.

We should accomplish God's purpose in our generation as did David (Acts 13:36). One important way to do this is to increase our numbers. This comes through the sharing of the gospel with those who do not know Christ. It also happens when two faithful homeschool graduates marry and produce, say, five or ten more faithful homeschool graduates! Such people contribute greatly to the cause of Christ.

In addition to increasing our numbers, however, we must increase our holiness. When unbelievers (and other believers) look at our lives, they should see something different from the general pattern of the world. The way we talk, the way we love, and the way we conduct ourselves should testify to the power of God. When unbelievers see the power of God working through our lives, they should be afraid — not of us, but of the Lord, the one whom we fear, and afraid of the judgment that will come upon them if they remain in disobedience to him.

Unrighteous leaders and shapers of society should be afraid that they will lose power and influence as righteousness spreads in the land. Believers should play such a prominent role in society that people think we have turned the world upside down (Acts 17:6). This effort begins with us as we seek to make a difference in the world.

2) Men are usually responsible for problems.

Joshua 5:2-9 describes the spiritual realignment that the Israelites made after their years of wandering in the desert. Those Israelites who had not died in the desert wandered long and lost many years in the promised land, because the men complained about God's provision and were too fearful to follow God into battle against the Canaanites (Num. 14).

Based on what I have seen and heard, I think that men are almost always responsible for the problems we face in families, churches, and societies. I can point that big finger because I am pointing it at myself, too.

We have child kidnappings and murders because men feed on filth. We have "unwanted pregnancies" because men do not control themselves. We have corporate scandals because men are greedy. We have broken families because men do not love and lead like Jesus. Men who do not have fathers setting a good example for them often follow in the footsteps of their fathers and fail to live as they should.

Yes, men are usually responsible for problems; but when they do their job well, God provides great blessings. Thank God that many men today are recognizing and pursuing their God-given responsibilities. We young men who are coming of age can start off on the right track.

I am thankful that my father has encouraged me by his example and teaching. He has given me a foundation of faith on which to build my life. However, whether or not your father or grandfather has diligently followed the truth, today is the day you can set your course. We men must stand up and fulfill our obligations to God and to those around us.

3) Following God's ways can be painful.

Since even talking about circumcision can be uncomfortable, do not think too much about how hard it must have been actually to circumcise a few hundred thousand men! This incident (Josh. 5:2-9) reminds us that following God's ways can be painful.

Many believers around the world suffer physical pain because of their faith. They are tortured and killed by their enemies. Most of us in so-called civilized countries do not face such treatment. We may hear an occasional mocking remark or face social stigma for our decisions, but we are not usually forced to bear on our bodies the marks of Jesus.

However, all of us face the deeper struggle and the deeper pain that comes from the internal war against sin. Even in the Old Testament, God wanted not just circumcision of the body, but circumcision of the heart (Jer. 4:4). That is what all believers, male and female, experience today (Col. 2:11-12). Plucking out eyes, cutting off of hands — these figurative expressions illustrate the painful decisions that we must make as followers of Christ.

For many parents in the modern homeschooling movement, the decision to homeschool was not automatic or easy. Older children who had attended public or private schools often wrestled with questions, too. Confidence grows with experience, however. As with other decisions in life, the first step is often the hardest. Once we submit to God, our path becomes easier to travel even if it is not easier to understand. Whatever God instructs, we should do, even when it is painful.

4) God wants to give us something better.

After the circumcising, the Israelites observed the Passover. The next day they ate of the produce of the land. The day after that, the manna stopped (Josh. 5:10-12).

Now the Israelites had not been especially pleased with the food God provided in the desert, but I imagine they got used to it. Some of them may have even been disappointed when it stopped. When God takes away something we love or depend on, however, he enables us to get on without it or he replaces it with something better.

The Israelites could have stayed in Egypt eating vegetables and slaving for Pharaoh. They could have stayed in the desert eating a regular diet of manna and quail. Instead, God wanted to bring them into a fruitful land flowing with milk and honey where they could work for themselves.

When you were younger, perhaps you did not always enjoy the educational assignments or chores your parents gave you. In many ways, though, the regimentation of childhood is easier to handle than the responsibility of adulthood. We cannot think and act and speak like children anymore. We must put childish ways behind us and accept the challenge of serving God as adults.

With the new responsibility comes new opportunity. We young adults have moved into a new phase of life. We do not enter this phase alone, however. Our parents can and should continue to provide godly counsel and correction, and we have a loving Father in heaven who is ready to provide for our needs as we continue walking by faith. God is giving us something better, and we should welcome the possibilities.

5) We should be on God's side.

Joshua chapter 5 closes with the powerful scene of Joshua meeting the man with a drawn sword. Joshua understandably asks whose side he is on. The man tersely replies "No" and says that he comes as captain of the host of the Lord (verses 13-15).

Nearly everyone wants God to be on his side. In all sorts of disputes among men, from sibling rivalries to cultural quibbles to church disputes to international wars, people on both sides of the debate think that God is on their side.

We can have the same attitude. Is God on my side because I do not go to public school? Is God on my side because I do not date? Is God on my side because I read the Bible? Is God on my side because I write inspirational songs and essays?

The question should not be "Is God on my side?" The question should be "Am I on God's side?" Yes, God is on our side in the sense that he is present to support and guide us. However, he is not on our side in the sense that he approves of everything we do and opposes everyone who disagrees with us.

When the messenger with the drawn sword met Joshua, God was preparing to lead the Israelites to victory over the Canaanites. The Israelites did not just happen to be on the right side. God chose the Israelites to be his own possession (Deut. 7:6-9) The Canaanites did not just happen to be on the wrong side. God was going to punish the Canaanites because of their wickedness (Lev. 18:24-25).

We should not expect God to be on our side just because we say the right things and go through the right motions. The Pharisees thought that God was on their side because of what they did, even though their hearts were far from him. We should do whatever is necessary to be on God's side, following his leadership and listening to his commands. If we have that motivation, then we will say and do the right things, too.

Going Forward

The generation of Israelites under Joshua's leadership went on to accomplish great deeds in God's name. They destroyed or drove out many of the Canaanites. They established a new society based on God's instructions. For a few decades they served the Lord well.

Then, sadly, a generation arose which knew not the Lord. The Israelites who had come out of the desert and conquered the land failed to pass on to their children the importance of following God. Their descendants went through multiple cycles of spiritual failure and restoration.

As we seek to chart a new course for ourselves and our future families, let us take a warning from Joshua chapter 5. Let us see the danger of falling from a spiritual high into a pit through negligence and indifference. We must not squander the inheritance we have received from our godly parents. We must not disappoint them and God by failing to pass on a multi-generational vision of faithfulness.

Let us take encouragement from this passage, too. Let us reflect on the wonderful things God has done for his people in the past. Let us consider the wonderful things God can do through us as we seek his way.

We are a generation of God's people coming of age and preparing to do our duty. The forces opposing us are powerful, but our God is even more powerful. We have received much, and much will be required of us. May we be found faithful.

Chapter 5

Honor Your Father and Mother

I live with two of the noblest persons I know. They have given me loving attention, education, and discipline. Looking back I realize that when problems arose, I was often at fault because I was wise in my own eyes rather than submissive to them. My father and my mother stuck with me through those difficult times of my immaturity. They are like that.

My parents did not receive the same type of training they have given me. Their parents and grandparents did not understand some of the principles that God has been pleased to show us. Among those close to us, we have seen the devastating effects of fornication, adultery, divorce, careless parenting, youthful rebellion, and suicide. We have seen the pain caused by unfaithfulness to the Lord and his ways.

By the grace of God, my parents have wrestled to get where they are through faith and prayer and trial and error. My parents made conscious decisions about our family life that put us on a new path. I honor them for it.

I honor my parents for knowing and loving the Lord. I honor them for teaching me to know and love the Lord. These are not abstract concepts in our family. My parents have taught and illustrated the importance of faithfulness by specific actions they have taken in our family life. They have distinguished themselves by their good deeds, deeds which praise them in the gates.

Family Time

My parents decided against preschool for good reasons. They wanted to keep us home as long as possible! However, with little knowledge of homeschooling, they enrolled us children in the nearby elementary school when the time came. Even then Dad and Mom appreciated the importance of family time, and we had many good times together.

We played games in the backyard and read books together. Church activities were a big part of our life since my father was a preacher. We have taken family vacations on a shoestring budget, eventually reaching all of the lower 48 states, Canada, and Great Britain (over a period of about 15 years). We developed the tradition of a weekly family night. Few things could disrupt our tradition of being together at home on Thursday nights for food, fun, and fellowship. I honor my father and mother for making family time a priority.

Homeschooling

Dissatisfaction with the schools increased as my parents' understanding of homeschooling increased, so in August before my sixth-grade year they decided to begin training us at home. We tried for two years to replicate at home the system and methods of the schools. As you may guess, that did not work.

In an effort to find a better way, we tried a local private school for one year. Despite the Biblical foundation of the school and the good intentions of the good teachers, social influences among the students were not positive. Our family life also suffered from the busy schedule we kept.

Dad's work took us from Illinois to Tennessee, and we gave the public schools another try because folks told us they were great. We quickly realized our mistake! The next year we returned to homeschooling, this time to stay.

As many other families have learned, experience with homeschooling deepened our understanding of what being a family means. Homeschooling is not something we do for a few hours a day instead of going to school. The word homeschooling is a convenient (and somewhat unsatisfactory) term for the full-time pursuit of spiritual, moral, social, and intellectual excellence for God's glory.

As this modern movement of parent-directed education continues to evolve, we may need to coin new words to describe our efforts. I do not particularly want to be known as a homeschooler. I want to be known as a disciple of Christ who puts my faith into practice in educational methods and everything else.

Home-based education in our family has even extended past high school, which I discuss in more detail in a later chapter. Many of the same issues that led us to reconsider primary and secondary schools led us to reconsider college, too. We especially doubted the wisdom of my going far away from home, living in an environment full of immature young people, and going into debt for a degree. I honor my father and mother for bringing us children up in the nurture and admonition of the Lord and for not kicking us out when we turn 18.

Preparing for Marriage

The Lord may have another path of service for any or all of my siblings and me, but we are preparing to serve him in our own households as husbands and wives.

Like many young couples in the '70s, Dad and Mom dated other people before they met and married each other. They recognize the foolishness of that practice now, and they have protected my siblings and me from the same activity. This is yet another area where they have questioned the accepted cultural practice and have sought a different path.

My parents are helping me to prepare myself spiritually, emotionally, relationally, and financially for the responsibility of marriage. When we believe that I am ready, I want them to help me choose a wife because I respect their judgment. I want to bring a young woman into their lives as a daughter-in-law whom they can love and appreciate without having nagging doubts about her suitability as my partner.

Just as the term homeschooling has acquired unnecessary baggage, so has the term courtship. Our approach to marriage preparation does not need a name, because I see it as a part of real life rather than an artificial procedure. I am glad my parents and siblings and I have learned this together. I honor my father and mother for helping us prepare for marriage with patience and purity.

Caring for Granddaddy

Our Mema died in January of 1999. She was the second wife of my grandfather, Wesley Notgrass. I never knew my father's mother; she died before I was born. Mema was the grandmother we knew. She had struggled with dementia during her final months, and Granddaddy Wes was worn out from caring for her at home.

His health was good at 84, but the trials of old age were coming upon him. He continued to live at his house for several months. We visited him and wondered what sort of help we should give him. After purchasing a new lawn mower, Granddaddy tried to take it out of his car trunk by himself! That understandably gave him a backache, and it was another sign that he needed assistance.

In August of that year, he moved from Columbia, Tennessee, to our home in Cookeville, Tennessee, about 100 miles away. Except for his four years, one month, and seven days in the army during World War II, he had lived his whole life in Columbia. Two of my sisters started sharing a room so Granddaddy could have a room of his own. Thus began our experience as a three-generation household.

Dad and Mom have taken him to the doctor, attended to his personal needs, managed his finances, cooked his meals, and otherwise tried to make his life comfortable and happy. My sisters and I have helped with these things, but Dad and Mom have led the way. Dad has given me a powerful example of a son caring for his father in his old age.

Mom gave much time to helping her father with his health needs before he died in 2003. Mom's mother has also needed help after the loss of her husband, and Mom shows kindness toward her elderly grandmother. Caring for the elderly in our families is a clear religious duty (1 Tim. 5:4). I honor my father and mother for doing it.

Caring for Children

In October of 2001, my parents welcomed three more children into our family through adoption. At ages 12, 9, and 7, they moved in with much emotional baggage. We used to think that caring for Granddaddy was hard. When my new siblings moved in, we realized how easy caring for Granddaddy had been!

During their troubled childhoods, these precious children had suffered things that we can hardly imagine. Their needs challenged us to put our faith into practice in new ways. We have had many tears and trials, but we have also had smiles and successes. The Lord is working on all of us.

Daycare centers, public schools, and nursing homes are three of the saddest places I know. I have not spent much time in prisons. They are sad, too, but at least the people trapped in them gave up their freedom by their choice of actions. Children and elderly people with special needs often do not have a choice about where they spend their days.

Caring for children and widows is a natural and logical extension of our home-based lifestyle that has developed around homeschooling. We cannot personally provide a home for every needy child. We cannot personally look after every widow. However, we can welcome some of the needy children into our home, and we can look after some of the widows and widowers, especially those in our own families. I honor my father and mother for showing me what pure religion is.

Working Together

For twenty-two years my father served churches as a minister and received wages from them for his labor. When Dad went to work, he usually went to the church building. Mom devoted much time there also to the preparation of Bible class material. We children were often at the building on days besides Sunday. We lived close to the church building, and we were involved in a limited way with Dad's work; but still we spent much time apart.

After Dad spent a few years working with a church in Tennessee, my parents began to develop educational materials for churches and families and to prepare them for publication. We began a part-time family business. In the summer of 1999, Dad left his preaching position so we could focus our efforts on this new work.

We did not get to have a home business because of fortuitous circumstances. We chose to have a home business because we wanted to work together at something we found useful and worthwhile. Dad and I have enjoyed more interaction with each other than we had in the past. We have worked in the same room on the same projects and have traveled together to several states meeting homeschoolers.

We have not become dot-com millionaires, but neither have we gone hungry or had to sleep outside. God has provided for our needs as he promises he will. Like farmers scattering seed, we have been working and waiting for a larger crop to allow me to establish a new household. We heard that new businesses need five years to grow strong. After five years of perseverance, we are beginning to see more fruit in ours!

Running a business takes much work. We have had long hours, confusing choices, and difficult experiences.

However, taking on those challenges together as a family has been a blessing. We have received other rewards for our effort, too, such as meeting many new friends and learning more about ourselves. I honor my father and mother for taking on the challenge of entrepreneurship.

Church Fellowship

In August of 2000, after much consideration, we decided to leave the 600-member congregation where Dad had last preached and to begin meeting with a group of saints in our homes. We maintained contact with members of our previous congregation. We did not consider our action a church split. Rather, we wanted to pursue more intimate fellowship with the Lord and with other believers by more closely following the example of the early believers.

We sing, study, pray, share in a fellowship meal including the Lord's Supper, and spend extra time together. Meeting in homes gives us a flexibility and familiarity with each other that is often missing in big churches. We do not have the overhead expenses of a building and grounds. Neither do we have a sign or a listing in the yellow pages. We are fellow believers encouraging each other in our daily walks.

Other families besides ours have hosted our Sunday meetings, but often they have taken place at our house. Dad and Mom have done the extra work of preparation and cleaning because they wanted to. Many people have not understood what we are trying to do. We have even had internal disturbances in our fellowship, as many church families have. Dad and Mom have moved forward, trying to do right. I honor my father and mother for taking the road less traveled when they think it necessary.

Facing Trial

The summer of 2002 brought a new challenge which my parents faced with fortitude. Dad and Mom went to a homeschool conference in Memphis, Tennessee. As they were working to hook up a trailer to our Suburban, the vehicle rolled back and pinned Dad to the trailer. Thanks to God, he was not killed. However, both of his wrists were shattered. His trip to the hospital that day began several months of medical treatment and therapy.

From the beginning, Dad knew that he could not change the situation by wondering "Why?" and complaining. At first he could do nothing with his hands. He underwent surgery to secure his bones with metal rods and pins and plates. Slowly he began to regain the use of his hands as he performed daily exercises to twist and stretch his forearms and fingers. The pain was terrible. The weakness was frustrating. The routine was monotonous. Dad accepted it as a trial which produced perseverance and character.

Now he is able to do almost everything he did before, including typing and writing and lifting. The stiffness and pain will probably never go away completely, and arthritis could make it worse. However, through this ordeal, Dad and Mom have exhibited the faith that has brought them through other challenges. They have shown the faith that has motivated them to live differently from the world. I honor my father and mother for working through this trial together.

My Ambition

You may think that your parents are too strict in some areas. You may think that your parents are not strict enough in other areas. You may think that you can run a household, manage money, and rear children better than your parents have done. I know, because I have wrestled with these thoughts, too.

Until we face these experiences ourselves, we will not know how prepared we are. Pointing out faults is easy, but showing appreciation is more valuable. Identify and appreciate the good things your parents have done for you. Show your thankfulness by honoring them.

Parents should want their children to go farther and do better than they have done. My parents know that they are sinners, and that keeps them humble. My parents also know that they are saints, and that gives them hope. Most importantly my parents know the Lord Jesus Christ, and they have encouraged me and shown me how to know him, too.

I have made it my ambition to honor my father and mother by imitating their example. Living my life to glorify the Lord of hosts may include various other activities, but right now I expect it to include taking a wife in purity and holiness, rearing faithful children, looking after people in need, working diligently for my daily bread, and fellowshiping with God's people.

Chapter 6

Why I Plan to Train My Children At Home

Some day in the not-so-distant future I may be gazing into the wrinkled face of a little baby. Not just any baby, mind you — my baby! Of course, it will be God's baby, one that he entrusts to me and to the wife he gives me. The possibility excites me. The possibility humbles me.

If God grants that desire of my heart, then I will begin the glorious task of rearing that child (and the others God sends to me) in God's way. Parenting is not a spectator sport. Foolish children do not automatically mature into wise, responsible adults. Some people say that parents are not important. People who say such things do not know what they are talking about!

Family-based learning rests on two basic premises for those who profess Jesus Christ as Lord. First, by the ordinance of God, who created the family, parents are responsible for training their children in his way. Second, by the power of God, who gives the Holy Spirit, parents are able to train their children in his way. God does not require the impossible. With him all things are possible!

Christ-centered home education is not merely one educational alternative. It is a requirement for believing families. Parents may choose to use other resources to assist them in their task, but they must remember their ultimate responsibility. As for me, I have seen enough of public and private schools to know that I do not want my children in those environments.

For five primary reasons, I plan to train my children at home: it allows liberty, it gives control over unlimited social interaction, it encourages redeeming the time, it promotes an integrated lifestyle, and it enables the provision of true teaching.

Liberty

All children are unique individuals who have special gifts from God. They do not belong to the government or to any other institution, and we should not force them into a prefabricated mold. When I train my children at home, I can chart our own course within the will of God.

My children need not follow the common track that most children follow. I can give them tools and encouragement to do uncommon things in the name of Christ. I do not want my children to keep up with their peers. I want them to excel far beyond their peers for God's glory. Home-based training gives parents the liberty to provide each child with the training he or she needs.

Better Social Interaction

Freed from the confines of school, my children and I can interact with a wide variety of people. We can enjoy visits with neighbors and relatives and other families. We can serve others in our church and community. We can work and travel and shop and conduct business. We can do whatever we want! And we can do it as a family, learning to show kindness and humility, to bear with each other, to forgive, and to love.

Critics of homeschooling often point to a supposed lack of socialization, but parents of school-bound children are the ones who should be concerned about negative socialization! I want to show my children godly examples, protect them from ungodly examples, and give them social skills for many situations. Home-based training gives parents control over unlimited social interaction.

Redeemed Time

Instead of postponing real life by attending an artificial school environment, I want my children to experience real life at home everyday. I feel sorry for children who spend eight hours at school, three hours at daycare, and ten minutes with Daddy. I intend for my family to work together, play together, study together, serve together, and pursue God's will together. Home-based training allows families to redeem more effectively the time God gives us.

Integrated Lifestyle

Life does not consist of distinct, blocked-off periods of time. I do not want my children to get into the habit of compartmentalizing their lives. I want them to see family, service, work, and education as interrelated under the lordship of Christ. Home-based training encourages and is itself a component part of an integrated lifestyle.

True Teaching

Any education that does not rest on the foundation of God and the Bible is an incomplete education. In all fields we should recognize God's authority and instruction. From infancy I want my children to learn the holy Scriptures which are able to make them wise for salvation through faith in Christ Jesus. The public schools obviously will not teach my children of Christ, and I cannot depend on anyone else to do it for me. Home-based training enables parents to invest much time in teaching their children God's truth.

Faithfulness

These goals will contribute to the pursuit of the one central focus for my future family: I am aiming for faithfulness. I pray that my wife and I, our children and their spouses, our grandchildren, and all of our descendants will be faithful to God forever (Deut. 5:29). This will not just happen, and I cannot achieve it on my own. By the grace and power of God, I will do what I can.

I look forward to training a faithful quiver-full of children who will fill their places in God's kingdom, treasure the Scriptures in their hearts, and follow Jesus Christ all of their days. That is why I plan to train my children at home.

Chapter 7

Home Education Past High School

State laws require school attendance until a certain age. They "allow" parents to direct this training at home, with guidelines varying from state to state. What happens when these requirements end? Does homeschooling stop and real life begin? How can we apply the principles of home-based, parent-directed education to young adulthood?

Our family has made some wrong turns, and we have not worked out all the details; but we are working toward our goal of multi-generational faithfulness by continuing to live together as a family.

When I was born, my parents assumed that I would go to college immediately after high school. They had attended college, and they figured that I would do the same. When I was starting kindergarten, my father wrote an article for a magazine giving advice from a father to a son who was going away to college. On vacation in the Northeast, we took a subway to Harvard. Our parents encouraged us by saying that we were capable of going to college there if we wanted to. Even after we started homeschooling, the assumption remained that I would attend a private university located in another state.

Our perspective changed over the years. When the time finally came for a decision about my training after high school, I entered the local state university and continued to live at home. That lasted for one semester.

I did fine academically, and I socialized well with the other students, but since I had tasted the goodness of home education, the educational approach on campus did not suit me. I like to study and explore on my own, so I left school with my parents' blessing.

Now we are engaged in a great learning adventure, and those past collegiate episodes are humorous to us. We are together developing a different approach for our family. My two oldest sisters and I have graduated from high school, but our education has not stopped. We are still learning, and we are still doing that primarily at home.

We are meeting other families who are charting their own course also, and that encourages us. Maybe your family has had similar thoughts. To encourage you, I want to share what we have learned and where we are going. Let us start by looking at what the Bible says.

What the Bible Says

Our culture assumes that children (so-called teenagers) will usually rebel against their parents and establish their own lifestyle, at least for a few years. Even though they denigrate the faith of their fathers and live in dissipation, their parents often refer to these children as "good kids." Perhaps the parents think that their children will settle down in their 20s or 30s, maybe when they start families of their own. Is this a good assumption?

The Biblical command to honor your father and mother (Ex. 20:12, Deut. 5:16) does not apply just to little children. Since most people are adults longer than they are children, it applies more to older people. Jesus used this command to rebuke Pharisees and scribes who did not care for their parents (Matt. 15:1-9). It surely applies to us young people who are in the midst of developing our vision, refining our skills, and considering marriage.

Even a quick study of Bible families reveals this startling trend: children frequently lived with their parents until they married! Exceptions exist, but the Biblical pattern appears simply to be that a man will leave his father and mother and cleave to his wife (Gen. 2:24).

In our supposedly enlightened age, we hear that parents hinder rather than help a child's development and that a child needs to be around other children in order to mature properly and to acquire necessary social skills. This philosophy contradicts the Biblical pattern.

God gives parents authority over children. Godly parents exercise this authority by diligently training their children in the truth. Grown children like me do not need less training than we did when we were younger. We need more advanced training in adult responsibilities. Many believers acknowledge this in theory, but they think that parents are reduced simply to giving advice when their children turn eighteen. The negative example of Eli and his sons should shock them into a deeper understanding of parental authority.

Eli's sons were worthless men who did not know the Lord (1 Sam. 2:12). As priests, they despised the Lord's offering by greedy theft, and they lay with the female helpers at the tabernacle (1 Sam 2:17, 22). Oh, well. Eli did the best he could. After all, boys will be boys. He gave them some indirect advice and wished for the best.

Eli's sons were men, not little boys. At least one of them may have been married at this time (1 Sam. 4:19). How did the Lord feel about Eli's laid-back parenting approach? He told Samuel that he was about to judge Eli's house forever. Eli knew what his sons were doing, but he did not rebuke them (1 Sam. 3:13).

If a five-year-old girl runs into a busy street, her mother should pull her back. If a ten-year-old boy starts using foul language, his father should rebuke him. If a fifteen-year-old girl wants to dress immodestly, her parents should restrain her from doing so. Why do people think that a twenty-year-old boy should be able to get away with avoiding his religious duties, squandering his (or his parents') money, marrying an unbeliever, or otherwise dishonoring his parents and his God?

A big part of our cultural aversion to parental discipline of older children is aversion to discipline in general. However, since believers have the right and responsibility to rebuke and restore other believers in sin, how much more do parents have the right and responsibility to rebuke and restore their own children, regardless of their age? Elders are supposed to have children who believe and who are not even accused of dissipation or rebellion (Tit. 1:6). If that is possible for elders, it is possible for all believers. It is what God expects.

The Bible teaches that parental authority lasts longer and extends more broadly than many people want to admit. This foundation provides a basis for moving on to practical considerations related to older children continuing to live at home.

Practical Considerations

Perhaps you are saying, "Okay, John, I know that my parents have authority over me. I follow Jesus, and I am not given to wild living. But when can I get out on my own?" I have had the same question! I have wondered about going off to college or getting an apprenticeship in another state. I wonder what it would be like. The idea seems attractive, even worthwhile at times. Calmer consideration brings me back to the conclusion that, for me right now, living with my family is the best way for me to prepare for my own family.

For financial, physical, relational, and spiritual reasons, I believe that living at home until marriage should be our default option. It is not the only option, but we should not leave home just to get away. If another opportunity for learning and serving comes our way, then we can weigh its merits with our parents and decide which path we should take.

Financial

In financial terms, living at home is a great deal: high quality room and board at a great price! Of course, it is not free. Besides working as a partner in our family business, I take out the trash, help with the dishes, and even make my own bed. I pay my share of "rent" from my family business proceeds. The price is small for the many benefits.

Having my own car is not essential. We arrange our travel plans to share the two cars we already have. I do not need my own Internet account, my own refrigerator, or my own lawn mower. By sharing these things, we can keep resources available for other things. Sharing requires patience and consideration of other's needs, and that is exactly what my future family will need from me. When I start my own family, I expect that my wife and I will acquire duplicate household goods, but even then sharing with our parents and others will be a good idea.

Disputes about finances lead to many domestic problems. Parents and children must work together to find a positive arrangement. Each family member has something to contribute and each member has varying needs. None of us needs much disposable income. (If you have money to throw away, I could find a good use for it!) The next chapter delves more fully into finances.

I could pay through the nose to live in a dorm or apartment and eat at a cafeteria and restaurants. I could run up debts for fancy toys and gimmicks. Yes, living at home is a financially-sound decision!

Physical

Living at home has physical benefits, too. The world is a dangerous place. Even suburbs and small cities are not immune to violence. For a young woman, home is the best place to protect her purity. Her father and brothers can be on guard against worthless men. For a young man also, home provides valuable physical protection.

One reason my grandfather needs company is in case he falls. Anyone can fall down the stairs or otherwise injure himself, however, so having other people around is nice. If I took a tumble down our staircase, I would be comforted to know that someone would be around soon to help me. The Scripture says that this is one reason why two are better than one (Ecc. 4:9-10).

Physical health is another consideration. Many college students and other "singles" are not known for their healthy lifestyles. Fast food and microwave dinners, late nights and lots of soda will take their toll on anyone. Making oneself overweight, sick, and tired is not fun in the long run. Living at home encourages physical health and provides physical protection.

Relational

We all need emotional intimacy, and living at home allows healthy intimacy. When a young woman moves off on her own and weakens the emotional bonds she has with her family, we should not be surprised when she seeks superficial romantic intimacy. It seems easy, and it is readily available. The same applies to young men. A man who wanders from his place is like a bird that wanders from her nest (Prov. 27:8).

My parents and I are learning how to relate to each other as adults. They are still helping me learn to be a man. I seek their guidance, but they also solicit my opinion on various matters that come up. Dad and Mom allow me great freedom in how I spend my time, but I am accountable to them for using my time well. They trust my judgment as a business partner to make decisions and to formulate plans. We bounce ideas around the office to arrive at collaborative solutions. We do not always agree, but dealing with differences is part of life.

Living at home also allows siblings to continue cultivating their relationships. Instead of spending lots of time with peers who will not be close to us in the future, we can spend time with our siblings. We want them to be close to us for the rest of our lives, so we need to keep building strong bonds. Close sibling relationships are beneficial now, and they will help us in the future as we move into new phases of life.

Family life reminds me that other people have needs. I cannot stay up all night, sleep all day, scatter my laundry through the house, disturb people with loud noises, or leave my things on the stairs. I must be considerate and responsible and helpful. I need to stay in practice so that I can relate well to a wife and children when the time comes. Living at home is good for my relationship skills.

Spiritual

In addition to financial, physical, and relational advantages, living at home provides spiritual benefits. How many young men and women forget their spiritual roots when they go off to college? They may eventually return to the faith, but only after years of wasted time. Not only do they hurt themselves, but they set a bad example for their future children.

Our families can hold us accountable in spiritual matters. Are we growing in the grace and knowledge of Jesus? Are we participating in fellowship with the body? Are we redeeming the time God gives us? If not, then our families are close by to remind us of our top priorities.

Living at home also helps us to fight temptation. Whether we are tempted to give away our heart before the proper time, to spend more money than we make, or to explore the dark side of the Internet, having family members nearby can lead us away from temptation.

Our parents have experience and wisdom to guide us in our spiritual journey. We are walking with them as fellow travelers, but they have been on the road longer than we. Brothers and sisters can also encourage each other as we go through the same emotions of growing up, face the same challenges to be patient and pure, and work toward the same goals of maturity and faithfulness.

Living It Out

Many factors favor living at home with our families before we start our own families. The goal of this approach is not to stifle individuality or to restrict our freedom. The goal is to prepare us better for our future roles. As the Scripture says, it is not good for man to be alone.

My grandfather was born in 1915 in Columbia, Tennessee. He graduated from high school in 1933 and did not go to college. He had a good job with the local newspaper during the Depression, and he continued to live at home with his parents. Between 1941 and 1945, he served in the U.S. Army. After the war, at age 30, he returned to Columbia. His new bride came over from England, and they set up their own household.

Not too long ago, this pattern was not uncommon. Our culture today is obsessed with education. Proponents apparently want children to go to school when they are three and stay until they are thirty. Instead of postponing real life in this artificial environment, we can enjoy real life with our families as we prepare to build our own families.

I have continued my personal study of computer science that I began around age 10 with a Commodore 64. That experience has prepared me to manage our office with five computers and two printers on a local area network. I have developed my skills on the piano and guitar and composed songs to share with others. I have started learning to play the violin, and it is a fun challenge! My understanding of history, government, and science has increased through the reading I choose. Writing and public speaking have honed my communication skills.

I do not have an expensive piece of paper to hang on my wall, but I trust that the result of my self-directed liberal arts education compares favorably with that of the majority of American college students. My parents have supported and helped me in my efforts to improve my mind and to develop my skills.

When I first left college, I loafed. I was looking for direction, but I was not looking hard enough. I got a job with a local business, and I did some independent work for a friend, but I had not focused my efforts.

During this period of pondering, I collected my thoughts on life and family into a personal manifesto that motivated me to move on. After we started our family business, Dad and Mom made me a partner. Now I manage our financial records, handle inventory and ordering, maintain our website, coordinate our event schedule, and take care of various other tasks.

Like most things in life, successfully living at home after high school does not require complicated rules and convoluted arrangements. We need simply to put our minds to the task and do it. We need to work responsibly, love generously, and seek first the kingdom of God and his righteousness.

Generation gaps are a detestable cultural invention. The world expects discord. We should pursue unity. The world demands personal independence. We should desire cooperation. The world disregards tradition. We should appreciate our godly heritage.

If you are a grown child like me, I encourage you to consider seriously the benefits of living at home until you marry. It is not necessarily easy. It requires a cooperative spirit from all involved. However, it is beneficial if approached in the right way.

Cultivate your relationship with your parents and siblings. Grow in wisdom and in favor with God and man. Practice for your future family by continuing to serve your current family. It is a good idea whose time has come again.

Chapter 8

So You Want to Be a Millionaire?

How often have you heard people imitate a certain game show theme song in a deliberative situation? How many question askers, letter turners, and prize demonstrators can you name? Before you reply, of course, make sure that you are giving your final answer. Whether we like it or not, television game shows have affected (infected?) our cultural experience.

What is so appealing about game shows? The thrill of competition excites us, and a few shows even feature a measure of intellectual stimulation. Winning is what game shows are all about, however — especially winning money and other cool prizes!

Money is not the root of all evil, but the love of money is (1 Tim. 6:10). When it becomes the thing we seek first, then we must recognize that we are on the wrong track. How should we disciples of Christ Jesus understand wealth, money management, and work? The Bible has much to say about these subjects. Since they are important to God, they should be important to us.

We need to understand the source of wealth and the battle between covetousness and contentment. We need to recognize the challenges that wealth brings and to recognize the supremacy of spiritual wealth over physical wealth. We need to study ethical considerations related to money and the relationship between the rich and the poor. We must also move to practical considerations about business, debt, giving, saving, and more.

The Source of Wealth

Economic theory may seem exceedingly complex to those of us without much experience in that area. You can easily get a headache trying to figure out how supply and demand fit into a global economy run by multi-national corporations funded by the capitalization of diversified financial interests. If haste makes waste, then what makes wealth? Does it come from the earth? From labor? From the acquisition of capital?

We can make it easy for ourselves by observing that wealth comes from God. Since the Lord made the earth and everything in it, he is the source of all forms of wealth. He distributes wealth to the people he has made. God blesses some of his followers with an abundance of material possessions, and others subsist on a limited, though sufficient, supply. Some unbelievers manage to amass great treasure, while many live in squalor. We cannot always understand the mysterious movings of the Almighty, but one thing that the rich and poor have in common is that the Lord made them all (Prov. 22:2).

As recipients of God's provisions, we can respond with only one of two attitudes. We can covet more, or we can be content with what we have. No other options are available. Neither can we blend these opposites into a unified attitude. Only one will accurately describe our understanding of wealth.

If we are covetous, we suppose that our own wisdom and strength have earned what we possess. We are not grateful because we believe that we got only what we deserved (or perhaps less than we deserved). We are not satisfied because we must always keep up with others. We are never happy because we always worry about what will happen tomorrow.

On the other hand, if we are content, we recognize that God is the source of our physical blessings. We are grateful because we know that we do not even deserve bread and water. We are satisfied because we need not compare ourselves with others. We are joyful in the Lord because we know what will happen tomorrow — we know that God will take care of us.

After we recognize the source of wealth, we must face the challenge of wealth. Applying the philosophical to the practical is where the rubber meets the gold.

The Challenge of Wealth

Wealth can be used for excellent purposes. Wealth can be used for terrible purposes. The challenge of wealth is to use it well and to keep it from consuming us. The battle between covetousness and contentment may seem especially fierce in our modern world of mass production and commercialism, but it has been raging for centuries.

The Old Testament strictly censures those who place their trust in riches. The New Testament contains many warnings against the love of money and the pursuit of sordid gain. Jesus himself provided much teaching on how we use our possessions.

Someone has been, will be, or currently is richer than we are now. We can always make the excuse that we are not really rich compared to that person. The challenge of wealth confronts everyone, however. Greed is idolatry whether you have a little or a lot.

We should not want to get rich. Did you catch that? We may become rich through hard work or inheritance, but getting rich should not be our goal. Sometimes I wish I had a million dollars. I would even settle for half that in cash! I tell myself that I would put it to good use, but why do I really want to get rich? So I will not have to "worry" about money? So I will not have to work so hard? My desires are not purely philanthropic.

God does not need me to make a lot of money so that I can give it away. He has many other channels besides me for distributing his good gifts. He will give me what I need to do what I can. A servant heart is more valuable than a fat wallet, so I should desire the former much more than the latter.

Paul gives us a specific warning about the challenge of wealth in 1 Timothy 6. Some people back then thought that living a godly lifestyle was a way to get rich. Sadly, things have not changed much! Living a godly lifestyle is a means of great gain, but only when accompanied by contentment. God will provide everything we need. At times that may include just basic food and covering.

Having sufficient material possessions is the reward for our diligence and obedience. It is not a right, and it should not be our goal. If we follow God so that we will get rich, then we are missing the point. If we follow God simply because we should, then we will be able to have and to enjoy what we need.

Rich people (and those who want to be rich) are tempted to trust in wealth as savior rather than in Christ. Wealth is attractive, and it can make people happy for a time; but wealth can vanish in a moment. It never provides lasting security.

Even if thieves do not break in and steal it, or moth and rust do not get it first, we know for sure that the rich man will not keep his wealth when he dies. We enter the world without a penny, and we leave it empty-handed, too. Neither money nor any physical possession can help us in the end.

Poor people are not free from the challenge of wealth. They have the temptation to be envious of richer people, and some of them try to improve their condition through theft or other dishonest means. However, since they do not have the same amount of contact with wealth, poor people can often recognize their need for the Lord more easily. Rich people may enter the kingdom of heaven with difficulty. Poor people may enter it with less strain, but entrance is still only possible with God.

The more we focus on spiritual wealth, the less we worry about physical wealth. The things in life that are most valuable are not silver and gold and the things they can buy. The things in life that are most valuable are the things that last — the things based on a wise and righteous lifestyle. The news media constantly remind us of the value of the fluctuating stock market. We must remind each other of the constant value of following God's plan.

You must decide what is most valuable to you. Think about your priorities. Would you rather have a million dollars or another child? Would you rather be CEO of a big corporation or be a hero to your children? Would you rather have a wall full of diplomas and awards or a heart full of wisdom and love?

These comparisons are not necessarily mutually exclusive; but too often, those who pursue physical wealth and honor among men do so at great spiritual expense. When you must make a difficult choice, are you ready to choose spiritual wealth over physical wealth?

True wealth comes from knowing the mystery of God's work in Christ Jesus. A simple meal in the modest dwelling of the righteous is much better than a lavish feast in the fancy mansion of the wicked. Even if our possessions are not numerous, even if they are confiscated or destroyed by disaster, we can be content because of God's wonderful provision for our spirits.

How We Get It, How We Use It

Financial considerations are often on my mind as I wonder how I can best prepare for my future needs and responsibilities. I do not expect to be like many other families, with my wife and me both working high-powered, high-paying professional jobs. Living in 21st-century America is expensive for most people. What can or should I do differently?

The Bible encourages us to make diligent plans based on wise counsel. Doing whatever feels right at the moment is not a healthy or efficient way to live. However, all of our plans are conditional on what the Lord wills. Some plans will go nearly as planned, while some will not get off the ground. God may allow other plans to succeed for a time; but if we do not keep our focus on him, then we will not enjoy the fruit of our labor (Luke 12:16-21).

Talking about things is much easier than doing them. Making plans is much easier than following them. Staying in bed and daydreaming is much easier than devoting myself to the tasks at hand, but I know that I must devote myself to those tasks. Talking and making plans and dreaming have a place, as does taking a break from our labor. We can only take a break from something we actually are doing, however. That means work.

Working

Because of Adam's sin, he had to earn his living by his sweat, fighting against the stubborn ground (Gen. 3:17-19). Compared to times past, relatively few people today, especially in industrialized countries, earn their living directly from the soil. Still, all of us must either work or hire people to work for us, and we are all still dependent on those who cultivate crops and manage livestock.

God redeems our work by giving us a purpose, a motivation, and a reward for our disciplined effort. Work and business and finance are not evil areas of life. We should not be ashamed of trying to do an honest job or to run an honest business. Nor should we feel the need to hide our labor behind a non-profit screen. Doing business and making a profit are a part of life on earth, and we should do them honestly.

The Bible mentions a wide range of occupations, including baker, banker, blacksmith, builder, carpenter, craftsman, designer, doctor, embroiderer, engraver, fabric seller, farmer, fisherman, fuller, gardener, goldsmith, government official, husbandman, lawyer, mason, merchant, metallurgist, metalworker, midwife, musician, nurse, perfumer, plowman, potter, quarryman, rancher, refiner, scholar, scribe, sea merchant, seamster, servant, slave, soldier, stone and gem worker, tanner, tentmaker, trapper, vinedresser, weaver, wet nurse, and winepresser.

Our society has developed new versions of these ancient tasks, but overall we still perform similar jobs related to eating, dressing, serving, building, learning, and governing. Some occupations, such as thief or prostitute, are inherently wicked, and some people perform respectable occupations in a wicked way; but we still have a great variety of suitable fields for our labor.

Whatever labor we engage in, we should do it well as though we were working for the Lord. Diligence is one of the virtues highly praised in the Proverbs, and laziness is as strongly condemned. Paying attention to our responsibilities shows that we do not take God's blessings for granted.

On the other hand, we can pay too much attention to work. Rising early and staying up late toiling for food is vain (Psalm 127). In one of Jesus' parables, people excused themselves from the banquet because they had to check their fields or try out their oxen (Luke 14). The Scripture says that he who does not work should not eat, so each of us should take care of the duties appropriate to our age and station. However, we must not let an intense pursuit of work interfere with our overall focus on serving God and man. We plant and water. God gives the increase, along with peace and rest.

If I work for someone else, I am a servant. I may be a temporary servant or an itinerant servant, but I am still a servant. Being a servant is not wrong, and it may be quite good in some circumstances. However, the Bible suggests that having a free occupation is better than being a servant.

The Old Testament contains three positive references to each man having his own vine and fig tree (1 Kin. 4:25, Mic. 4:4, Zech. 3:10). Paul told believing servants (a term including both voluntary and involuntary) that they should not worry about their condition, but they should take advantage of freedom if possible (1 Cor. 7:21).

Having a free occupation is not necessarily easier than working for an employer. Business owners work for their customers! Employees have one boss (or one chain of command), but self-employed individuals must respond to the wishes and needs of multiple people in their customer base. Each option has challenges and opportunities, so each of us must identify good ways to use the talents God gives to serve him effectively.

Giving

We work to earn our daily bread. Instead of passing our days in idle pleasure, we spend them in diligent effort, and God rewards the labor of our hands with the fruit of that labor. We also work so that we can give to those in need — a goal of perhaps equal importance (Eph. 4:28).

Abraham provides the first example of tithing when he gave Melchizedek a tenth of the spoils he had captured (Gen. 14:20). Jacob promised to give the Lord a tenth of everything the Lord gave him (Gen. 28:22). The law given to Moses codified God's instructions concerning the tithe.

The law describes different aspects of the tithe in different passages. The Levites received tithes to provide for their needs since they did not have an inheritance in Israel (Num. 18:21-32). Part of it went to help the poor (Deut. 26:12-15). The people enjoyed some of it by eating it as a feast before God when they brought it to him (Deut. 14:22-29).

The New Testament says much about giving, but not much about tithing. I do not think that believers today must give 10% of their income to worthy causes. We can give more! Charity is more than alms, but the disposition of our treasure shows the inclination of our hearts.

One of the loveliest word pictures of Jesus that has stuck in my mind for many years is that from Luke 6:38: Give and it will be given to you, good measure, pressed down, shaken together, running over, poured in your lap!

We can discuss whether we give before taxes or after taxes, whether we give based on our gross or our net, and who should receive our donations. By chasing side issues, we can easily miss the point. Are we trying to see how little we can give or how much we can give?

A few people might get into trouble by giving "more than they can afford," but most of us are not in that danger. Paul praised the Macedonians who gave out of their joy and poverty even beyond their means. They considered it a favor to be able to give (2 Cor. 8:1-4).

We are God's investment managers. He created everything. He owns everything. He entrusts a certain amount to our care, and we are supposed to put it to good use. Giving to those in need and helping good causes go farther are among the best investments we can make. The old saying that "God helps those who help themselves" could be worded better "God helps those who help others." When God demands an accounting from us, we can show him the good return we made by the lives we touched.

Investing

Socially-conscious investing is a trendy activity. Many investors try simply to get the best return on their money, but others make some kind of critical analysis of the moral value of their investments. Trying to figure out where every dollar ultimately goes is an impossible task, but I agree that we should be attentive and careful, seeking not to offer direct support to entities that are exploitive and corrupt. We do not want to earn deceptive wages or to get deceptive deals. Even more important than socially-conscious investing, however, is social investing. By social investing, I mean investing in people.

Your 401(K) may be small or non-existent. Your stock portfolio may be as disorganized as it is diversified. You may have more money in music CDs than you have in bank CDs. However, if you are investing your time and energy and money in people, then you are doing well, wonderfully well.

Parents who have children have a diversified investment portfolio in their own home. Children come in two varieties, boy and girl, and they have different dispositions and talents. An investment in the life of a child has an unlimited rate of return. Every child trained in the Lord has the opportunity to affect the lives of innumerable people through his or her future family and work in the world.

All of us have opportunities to sow the seeds of love and reap the harvest of righteousness in the lives of other people. Those who are rich in the world's goods must also be rich in good deeds. If having wealth enables them to do more good, then they are indeed blessed. If they are not rich toward God, however, then all of their careful planning and all of their projected returns will be worthless.

A good man leaves an inheritance for his grandchildren (Prov. 13:22). Paul comments on the idea that parents should save up for their children rather than vice versa (2 Cor. 12:14). As we learn from other passages, a child who is given a head start financially must also be given a heart start spiritually. Children and grandchildren need the heirlooms of faith and holiness more than they need anything made of wood or gold or brick. Jesus warned a man, who was concerned about his inheritance, that life does not consist of our possessions, no matter how many we have (Luke 12:13-15).

We should be as wise as the ant in preparing for tomorrow, and we should be as careless as the birds in enjoying today. How do we strike a proper balance between those attitudes? Saving for a particular purpose is wise, such as saving for a car, a house, a trip, or the financial winters that come. Having large amounts of money lying around for nothing in particular seems unnecessary, however. What God has given, God can give again.

Before we consider lending and borrowing, let me point out that making and accepting investments is different from taking out loans and mortgages. When two parties share the risk in a business enterprise by pooling their resources and talents, they should share in the profit (or loss). One person may invest money and the other may invest time, but this is a partner-partner relationship rather than a master-slave relationship. Believers who want to find a good use for their extra money might consider helping other believers get started in their own free enterprises.

Lending and Borrowing

A large percentage of church-going people are in debt for a house, a car, a college education, a vacation, or something else. A few might try to argue that this situation is good for the economy or that it provides tax benefits, but surely most of us would agree that we would be better off without our debt burdens. We may like to think that our borrowing is all for a good cause, but deep down we should realize that generally it supports our hankering for bigger and better toys.

According to the Bible, being able to lend is a blessing, while having to borrow is a curse. The Scriptures seem to assume that generally the only ones who will borrow are the poor (Ex. 22:25, Lev. 25:35) and the wicked (Ps. 37:21, 109:11; Prov. 20:16; cf. Deut. 24:10-13). Our modern consumer culture teaches us to get what we want right now, even if we have to borrow for it. Is Paul's simple injunction to owe no man anything but love just too old-fashioned (Rom. 13:8)?

The Proverbs contain several colorful warnings against going surety for someone else. If you go surety for someone else, you might have to pay the loan back. If you "go surety" for yourself, you will have to pay it back! How far should we take that line of reasoning? The Proverbs tell us that the borrower is slave to the lender, and we have seen before that believers ought not be in slavery if they can be free.

What is wrong with borrowing? First, borrowing robs us of the freedom to give. Those who are enslaved to a lender cannot give freely because they are obligated to repay their debt. Second, borrowing suggests to the world that God is not meeting our needs. God has promised to supply our physical needs if we trust him and seek first his kingdom. Does he need us to supplement his provision by taking out loans and repaying them with interest, especially to unbelievers? Instead of borrowing, we should be ready and willing to lend, without expecting repayment.

The one exception I see to the Biblical teaching against borrowing is the case of a poor believer who is living faithfully and working according to his ability. If he lacks food and covering, then we, his brethren, have the duty to help him gladly. In this case, God's provision comes through the church. If the needy person is later able to repay, that is fine; but we should lend at no interest without expecting even the principal in return (Deut. 15:1-11, 23:19-20; Ps. 15:5; Prov. 28:8; Luke 6:34-35).

Lest you think that our family has mastered the art of financial management, we are still serving a lender with a home mortgage, too. However, our attitude toward finance has changed over the years, as has our attitude toward many things in life. We want to get out of debt, because debt binds us. It holds us down. It disables us from getting where we want to go.

Credit is ready and waiting everywhere we look. Credit card companies bombard us with offers for new pieces of plastic. We can buy furniture, computers, and virtually anything else now and pay later (through the nose). Even auto makers have expressed their willingness to give us a new vehicle without charging usury! Once we start, however, stopping the cycle of debt is hard. To owe no man anything but love is a wonderful approach to finance.

Building Community

Understanding basic money principles from the Bible is easy. Putting them into practice is more difficult. Restoring a sense of community is one of the most important projects for which I sense a need. The ancient Israelite society, the first century church, and many Biblically-influenced groups up to modern times have enjoyed a communal (not communist) lifestyle that many folks like me have not experienced. How, in economic terms, can we apply Paul's instruction to do good to all, especially to those of the household of faith (Gal. 6:10)?

This effort must start in the family. Parents and children should cooperate to advance the interests of the family. While we children are living at home, we likely do not need much discretionary income. My personal expenses are not great, so much of my work is not directly compensated. A portion of my earnings goes toward current household expenses, and most of the rest is left invested in our business.

One major family goal is for me to be able to start my own household with a debt-free residence. If I can establish a new household without bringing a load of consumer or student debt and build a house without a mortgage, I will be able to live and give freely, without the financial burden faced by many of my peers.

Everything done for the good of the family is valuable, whether or not it generates income. Washing dishes is not less important than crafting a product for the family business. The father, mother, and each child should contribute something based on his or her position and talents. Family members should show appreciation for what each other member does.

Children can help their parents achieve good goals by contributing their energetic labor to the family economy. Parents can help their children achieve good goals by teaching them financial principles and giving them work experience. By working together, the end result will be better than what any one could achieve alone.

Can we broaden the application of these principles to the larger community? I do not want central government planning. That has proven itself to be impractical at best and dangerous at worst. Even at the local level, utopian communities do not last long following the idealistic patterns with which they start out. What I am imagining is a group of people voluntarily working together for their common good.

Families can work with other families to advance the interests of their community. They can support local businesses. They can have barn-raisings and similar activities that reduce costs and improve relationships. Family businesses can cooperate with other family businesses to improve production, distribution, and management. These are thoughts-in-process that our family has chewed on.

My main point with the concluding section of this chapter is to consider how money management is about more than how I manage my money for myself. Instead of just thinking about what I want, what I have, and what I spend, I should consider what others want, what others have, and what others need. "Love your neighbor" and "Do unto others" are positive commands that require us to look out for the interests of others.

If you want to be a millionaire, expect to be disappointed. Either you will miss that mark and be let down, or you will achieve it and realize that money cannot buy what you want most of all. If, instead, you appreciate what God has given you and use it well, expect to be satisfied. Seek first God's kingdom, and you will have more than you deserve.

Chapter 9

Being Different

Speaking of money, I have never been a big shopper. Going to the store was bearable if I could find a place to read or at least peruse the electronics section. These days I do not even like to go to the store. Advertisements show things that should not be seen in public. Magazines in the checkout line flaunt their perversity. Real live human beings walk around like the emperor in the story — they have nothing on!

We live in a culture intoxicated by the lust of the flesh. Skin is in, and the promotion of sensual pleasures is all around us. How can we as followers of Christ stand firm against this trend? We need to honor God with our bodies. We need to recognize that our choices have consequences. We need to think differently, dress differently, and act differently.

Many of the thoughts in this chapter are taken from the letter of 1 Corinthians. There Paul is instructing believers in how they should conduct themselves in an immoral culture. His lessons are immediately applicable to us today. If you have not read it recently, I encourage you to read Paul's entire letter. I cannot improve on his message, but I will highlight ideas that stand out to me.

Think Differently

We humans have limits. We cannot be everywhere or see everything simultaneously. We cannot automatically follow each option before us to its ultimate conclusion (logical or not). God's wisdom is high above ours. Even his foolishness is wiser than we are. Therefore, we cannot depend on our own perceptions and our own thought processes to lead us in the right direction.

In his mercy, God has given us guidance to help us make decisions. We must set our minds on this higher wisdom. We must set our minds on things above. If my mind is not set on things above, it will necessarily be set on things below. If my mind is set on things below, I will much more easily fall into the sensual traps that wait all around me.

Though we humans have limits, we also have great capabilities. We can recognize sin and identify it as such. We can know right and wrong. We can make moral decisions. Our motivation in everything should be to glorify God. Our love for him and our love for other people must modify our behavior. It must compel us to be different from those who love only themselves.

People in the world are childish in their thinking, but they are experienced in evil. The Lord calls us to be mature in our thinking, but to be inexperienced ("babes") in evil

(1 Cor. 14:20). Because we are surrounded by immoral influences, and because we so often give in to them, we must make constant effort to unlearn bad habits and to learn good ones.

The events of the past are examples to us. Scripture records selected events for our instruction. Temptations to immorality may seem hard to avoid today, but they have been common to man throughout history. With each one comes a way of escape. We must learn to identify those routes of escape so that we are not trapped in our selfish lusts. We must think differently from the world around us.

Dress Differently

Even at events for homeschooling families, the attire of some of the young women (and some of the older women) shocks me. If the Lord gives me a family, I intend to help my wife and children present themselves to the world with becoming attire.

We do not need complicated rules about clothing, but we do need thoughtful consideration. We should not blindly accept the fashions thrust upon us by the world. One practical consequence of our different perspective on life should be a difference in the way we dress.

I want my wife to keep herself covered in public from her neck to her knees. I want her to reserve that part of her body for me. I am not just being selfish. I do not want other men to be uncomfortable in my wife's presence, as I often am in the presence of other women. I also want each of my daughters to keep her body covered for her future husband.

I want to protect the women in my family from drawing inappropriate attention to themselves by helping them to consider a few simple questions. Does this outfit expose parts of the body that should be covered? Do these clothes fit too tightly or hang too loosely (such as when you bend over)? Do your undergarments show through these clothes?

Modest dress applies to men, too. Stripping for exercise or work is not necessarily cooler, and it is not becoming. Exposing one's upper body is not necessary to prove one's strength. Questions for me and my sons include these: Am I trying to show off my body with this choice of attire? Does my appearance come across as haughty or grungy? Our attire (or lack thereof) should not draw undue attention to us. It should be neither erotic nor exotic.

When the Bible speaks of nakedness, one of the primary reasons for it is poverty. Paul says that he was hungry, thirsty, and naked as a servant of Christ (1 Cor. 4:11). I have not yet gathered the courage to approach someone dressed immodestly and say, "I'm sorry you cannot afford more clothes. Can I help you buy some?" Do you think such an approach would be effective?

May a daughter of God walk around in public wearing a tank top and short shorts? "All things are lawful," but this is most certainly not profitable (except for the big-name clothing companies, which charge twice as much for half the clothing). Some parts of the body need to be covered (1 Cor. 12:23-24). Our bodies belong to the Lord.

Does dress seem like an insignificant issue compared with promiscuity and other perversions? It may seem so; but dress, the appearance we present to the world, reflects the way we think and influences the way we act.

I am not calling for powdered wigs and leggings and corsets and hoop skirts. I am calling for decency. As we consider what to wear, we should ask, "How can I honor God with my body and help those around me to think and to act with purity?"

Act Differently

Our fleshly lusts are not much different from the animals. We see, we want, we take. Unlike the animals, however, we can control our lusts through the Holy Spirit. God teaches us self-control. Such training is not easy. We must buffet our bodies, making them our slaves.

Our actions affect others. A little leaven leavens the whole lump, so we must clean out the old leaven. Judgment must begin with the household of God. We may not be able to change the fashions on Madison Avenue this year, but we should be able to do something about Main Street Church.

The most important thing is not what we want. We are not called to seek our own good but rather the good of our neighbor. We should do everything in love, giving no offense to anyone as far as it depends on us.

Cohabitation before marriage (and old-fashioned one night stands) are common. Adultery captures its prey among the high and low. States are granting same-gender partners special recognition, if not full marital rights. The U.S. Supreme Court ruled against a Texas statute prohibiting sodomy. The Canadian House of Commons passed a bill to prohibit "hate speech" against people who have certain sensual orientations. This is what we are up against in our day and time.

In addition to thinking and dressing differently, we must also act differently. Fornication, adultery, and sodomy do not just happen. They are the final steps in a journey of compromise and corruption. Those who practice such things will not inherit the kingdom of God. We need to recognize sin and repent of it, not rejoice in it.

If we are in Christ, then Christ is in us. Our bodies are a temple of the Holy Spirit. We have been purchased with a price, and we must no longer act as if we belong to ourselves. We must flee immorality.

How sad that our culture has denigrated innocence and purity and encouraged immorality and perversion — from the abuse scandals in the Roman Catholic Church to the campaign for special rights for sodomites and lesbians to commonplace cases of corrupt behavior. Instead of fleeing immorality, many have welcomed it with open arms. God's people must be different. We must avoid even the appearance of evil.

Conclusion

Will we allow ourselves to be swept along with the tide of indecency, or will we wade against it? We need to mend our hearts and not just our garments. God wants us to do more than put on extra fabric. God wants us to put on a new attitude. If we have a different attitude from the world, our actions will necessarily be different. Let us be on the alert, stand firm in the faith, and act like men and women of God.

Chapter 10

What God Joins Together

Imagine that you are getting ready for an eight-hour road trip. Your destination is a new one to you, so you are excited and a little scared. You want to prepare yourself and your vehicle properly so that the trip will go as smoothly as possible. You want to get a good night's sleep before the trip so that you will be fresh and alert. You need to bring a few resources with you, such as a map to show where you are going, food and drink to keep you strong, and a spare tire just in case. You must fill your car with gasoline, check the oil and tires and brakes, and buckle your seat belt. You will also want to know how to drive!

If we put this much preparation into a simple day's drive, how much more should we prepare for the lifelong journey of marriage? The beauty and importance of this divine union demand our careful attention. Many couples try to run a healthy relationship on the fumes of romantic attraction. When their marriages blow a tire or lose direction, all too often they look for another ride.

If the Lord wills, I plan to build a faithful and fruitful marriage for his glory. The world has developed a pattern for making families, and the results are often terrible. Marriage between believers and unbelievers, fornication, adultery, and divorce — these have detrimentally affected many families. Our family has pondered together how to develop an alternate approach that more effectively guards against them.

The best way to prevent the defilement of marriages is to start well at the beginning. Laying a good foundation is essential to the strength of the final structure. Where can we learn how to build good marriages?

The Source

We should run to the Bible for this guidance. It is the fountain of wisdom in all things pertaining to life and godliness. The instructions are there; we must take them, study them, and apply them. Some may fear that adherence to God's guidelines regarding male-female relationships will take the fun and spontaneity out of romance. We see all around us, however, that sin and selfishness take the real joy out of romance. We should want something different from the way of the world!

I decided several years ago not to follow the common path to marriage of experimentation and emotional selection. I have learned from Scripture and from wise counselors how to avoid problems that many young people bring on themselves. As in many areas of our family life, this is one we have had to grow into. We have struggled with uncertainty and missteps, but we are glad that we do not have to plan dates on Friday nights.

The Goal

I am seeking a godly wife who will help me fulfill God's commands. I believe that God knows whom I will marry, but I am not convinced that he will one day whisper in my ear, "That is the girl for you." He may do that or whatever he wishes, but unless he chooses to give me such a special revelation, I must select a wife based on wise application of the teaching of Scripture.

As I discussed in an earlier chapter, Scripture teaches us what God's will is. He has provided examples and instructions showing me what I need to know about selecting a virtuous wife. I believe that God works through circumstances and through other people to guide us in the right way. However, in my experience, such guidance usually becomes apparent after the fact.

If I were seeking a wife out of selfish, fleshly motivations, I could probably find a match quickly and easily. The principle of reaping what you sow applies to marriage, too (Gal. 6:7). I am not worried about finding "the one." I trust God to provide her at the proper time. If and when I marry, I will thank God for providing a prudent wife (Prov. 19:14). I will rejoice in finding "a good thing" and in obtaining the Lord's favor (Prov. 18:22).

Purposes of Marriage

Marriage is not an end in itself. We know that in the resurrection people neither marry nor are given in marriage (Matt. 22:30). Paul taught that remaining unmarried was good and sometimes even better than marrying (1 Cor. 7). When the disciples marveled at Jesus' teaching on divorce, he replied that not everyone could accept his statement, but only those to whom it was given (Matt. 19:11).

Some disciples would do better not to marry, and all of us should wait to marry until we are ready to serve God well as a husband or wife. If you decide to serve God without marrying, you will do well. Serve him faithfully. Parents, if your child decides to serve God without marrying, do not assume that something is wrong with you or with your child. Encourage him or her to serve God faithfully. Some have the gift for marrying and some for not marrying, and each of us should walk in the way God has provided (1 Cor. 7:7,17).

If we do choose marriage, our goal should not be personal gratification. Instead, we should seek to glorify God, to be a living parable, to enjoy holy intimacy and to produce godly offspring, and to disciple the nations.

To Glorify God

Marriage is good because God created it (Gen. 1:26-31, 2:18-25), and we should always honor it (Heb. 13:4). Agur declared that the way of a man with a maid was too wonderful for him. It was something he did not understand (Prov. 30:18-19). When God described the coming blessedness of Zion, he said that the land would be called "Married" (Beulah) rather than "Desolate." God would rejoice over his people as a bridegroom rejoices over a bride (Isa. 62:4-5). Jesus spoke positively of marriage (Matt. 19:4-12), and he even participated in a wedding banquet (John 2:1-12). Those who forbid marriage are wrong, for it is a good thing created by God (1 Tim. 4:3-5).

The prime motivation for every activity we undertake should be to please and to honor God. Nothing else compares to living for his glory. Preparing for marriage and living as husband and wife are not exceptions, so our chief ambition in marriage should be to glorify God.

To Be a Living Parable

Our marriages paint a picture for the world to see. Strong marriages beautifully illustrate the relationship between Christ and the church. Bitter and divisive unions present a dark caricature of that relationship. Marriage is an exclusive covenant between a man and a woman. God uses the marriage bond in both the Old and New Testaments to illustrate his relationship with his people.

Failure to honor the marriage bond produces terrible results. When Nathan confronted David concerning his sin with Bathsheba, Nathan said that by his deed, David had given the Lord's enemies an occasion to blaspheme (2 Sam. 12:14). David and Bathsheba's first child died because of their sin.

Our behavior both as unmarried people and as husbands and wives reflects either positively or negatively on our Lord. We should be living parables for the world, examples that illustrate the purity of God, the servant authority of Christ, and the gentle submission of the church, so that the word of God may not be defamed (Tit. 2:5).

To Provide Intimacy and To Produce Godly Offspring

God made humans with a desire for intimacy. He made a helper for Adam because it was not good for him to be alone. He designed Adam and Eve for spiritual, emotional, and physical intimacy with each other. Within a few generations, their descendants corrupted God's original design with polygamy and other perversions.

Because of immoralities, Paul acknowledged the propriety of each man having his own wife and each woman having her own husband. Only marriage gives a man and woman freedom to enjoy full intimacy with each other (1 Cor. 7:2-5,9). The husband gives himself to his wife for her good, and the wife gives herself to her husband for his good. They should not deprive each other of intimacy or take advantage of each other for personal gratification (Gen. 38:8-10).

Physical intimacy is the means by which God has provided for the growth of the human population. God commanded the first couple to be fruitful and multiply, to fill the earth and subdue it (Gen. 1:28). The fulfillment of this command depends on the obedience of future generations, and additional Scriptures confirm that this injunction applies to us (see the next chapter).

God formed the earth to be inhabited (Isa. 45:18). His purpose for his people is not merely the propagation of the human race, however. He wants his people to train their children as a warrior sharpens his arrows for battle (Ps. 127:4-5), and he wants those children to live such godly lives that the enemy may be put to shame, having no evil thing to say about us (Tit. 2:8).

To Disciple the Nations

Families adorn the doctrine of God our Savior by their godly lifestyle and good deeds. By God's grace, we can lead other households to faith in Christ as they see the health and strength we derive from him. Once those families are converted, they need older men and women to train them in Biblical family living (Tit. 2:1-5). Individuals compose families and families compose nations, so helping one helps the others.

This process continues the spread of the gospel throughout the earth. As new congregations of believers are established, they need leaders who have proven themselves by managing their households well (1 Tim. 3:4-5,12). As new generations arise, they, too, should know the holy Scriptures which are able to give them the wisdom that leads to salvation through faith in Christ Jesus (2 Tim. 3:14-15). Parents are responsible for training their children to keep the way of the Lord so that the children will train their children to follow the same pattern.

As I have mentioned before, my prayer and goal is that my wife and I, our children, our grandchildren, and all of our descendants will be faithful to the Lord forever. I want to take the truth my parents have taught me and tell it to the next generation, so that even the children yet to be born will continue the pattern of faithfulness. Together we can spread the good news among the nations.

Preparation

Young man, you desire a good thing if you desire to be a husband and father someday. Young woman, you desire a good thing if you desire to be a wife and mother someday. Noble is the mission of glorifying God by illustrating the gospel, by raising up godly seed, and by spreading his kingdom in the earth. You may not be ready to marry now, but you can rightly prepare yourself to marry in the future. Remember that your hopes and dreams are in God's hands. You should live with the belief that only if the Lord wills, will you do this or that (James 4:15).

Remember your Creator in the days of your youth (Ecc. 12:1). God deserves your primary affections whether you marry or not. In Jesus' parable of a dinner, one man excused himself by saying he had married a wife and thus could not come (Luke 14:20). Jesus continued his teaching by saying that for a man to be his disciple, he must hate his parents and wife and children and family and even his own life (Luke 14:26).

Marriage will bring extra challenges and responsibilities that could distract you from following Christ (1 Cor. 7:32-35). Do not let your desire for marriage interfere with your service to God now. Remember to delight yourself in the Lord, waiting for the fulfillment of your heart's desire in his time and in his way (Ps. 37:4).

A Husband's Roles

Loving His Wife

When Abraham's servant returned with a wife for Isaac, Isaac brought her into his mother's tent, took her as his wife, and loved her (Gen. 24:67). Isaac knew how to treat his wife, even though they barely knew each other. He loved her.

The earth cannot bear up under an unloved woman when she gets a husband (Prov. 30:21,23). Leah knew the pain of being "hated" by her husband Jacob. She longed for him to love her, to be attached to her (Gen. 29:31-35). So we have the plain instruction in Scripture: Husbands, love your wives (Col. 3:19).

This love is not a fleeting attraction based on appearance or emotion. The love demanded of husbands is a generous, sacrificial love based on commitment. As

Christ loved the church and gave himself up for her, so must a husband love his wife. He must treat her body as his own body, nourishing and cherishing, not abusing (Eph. 5:25,28,29). A husband must relate to his wife tenderly and with understanding, recognizing her precious status as a weaker vessel. For his prayers to be effective, he must grant her honor as an heir of God's grace together with himself (1 Pet. 3:7).

Faithfulness to your wife is a vital component of your love for her. If you marry the girl you "loved" as a young man, then frustrations and disagreements in marriage may tempt you to leave the union later on. However, if you love sincerely the girl you marry, then you will do everything you can to make your union blessed.

Your wife must know that she is the desire of your eyes (Eze. 24:16) and that you will never leave her or forsake her. God has promised to be faithful to us (Hos. 2:19,20; 2 Tim. 2:13), and husbands must be faithful to their wives (Mal. 2:10-17).

Leading His Wife

According to Numbers 30, a husband leads even when he does nothing. A believing husband must take an active role in leading his wife and children. The Persians were technically right in saying that every man should be the master in his own house (Est. 1:20-22), but we know that the godly man uses his authority as master to serve and to bless those under his hand, not to abuse or to embitter them.

God told Eve that her husband would rule over her (Gen. 3:16), and Paul clearly tells us that the husband is the head of his wife (1 Cor. 11:3, Eph. 5:23). Again, the godly husband will exercise this headship in a humble, gentle manner, but he must take his position seriously.

For instance, if a wife makes a rash or improper commitment without her husband's authority, he can annul that commitment when he hears about it (Num. 30). A husband should teach his wife when necessary (1 Cor. 14:34-35) and lead her away from sin (which Adam failed to do, Gen. 3:6-12). The husband should direct his family in keeping the Lord's way (Gen. 18:19, 1 Sam. 1:21), not leaving that responsibility to his wife (cf. Ex. 4:24-26).

Perhaps the most important part of a husband's leadership is establishing a vision for his family. Where do you plan to lead your wife, young man? Do you want to travel around the world as missionaries? Do you want to establish a farm in the country? If you do not know where you are going, then you will not know when you get there. Develop goals for your family that reflect Biblical principles and that encourage faithfulness. Then lead your family in executing them as God allows.

Providing for His Wife

Physical provision perhaps comes to mind first in this area, and a husband does owe his wife food and clothing (Ex. 21:10-11, 1 Tim. 5:8). He should also give her physical protection (good example, Gen. 33:1-3; bad example, Judg. 19:25) and the same tender care he gives his own body (Eph. 5:28-30).

A husband also owes his wife physical intimacy (Ex. 21:11, 1 Cor. 7:2-5; cf. 2 Samuel 20:3). If the adulterous wife in Proverbs 7 was telling the truth about her husband (7:19), then his long journey apparently left his wife with unfulfilled desires. She was wrong to be unfaithful, but he may have been in the wrong, too.

A husband should not frequently live apart from his wife, even for mission work (1 Cor. 9:5). Sometimes the husband will need to honor his wife by restraining his desire for intimacy (Matt. 1:25, 1 Cor. 7:5).

Young man, when you find a wife, work hard to make her happy (Deut. 24:5). Praise her and thank her and encourage her (Prov. 31:28-29). Let her find rest and security with you (Ruth 3:1).

Fathering His Children

Since fruitful multiplication is a purpose of marriage, young men should also prepare to be fathers. God may choose not to bless you and your wife with children through your union. You should be willing humbly to accept that occurrence. Perhaps you will be able to adopt children and mentor other young men and women.

God places primary responsibility for child training on the father (e.g., Gen. 18:19, 1 Sam. 3:13, Mal. 4:6, Eph. 6:4, Col. 3:21, Heb. 12:7-11), though the mother obviously plays an important role (e.g., Prov. 1:8, 2 Tim. 1:5). Bringing children up in the discipline and instruction of the Lord requires years of diligent effort, but since you do not want your children to wander through life in doubt and disbelief, you must train them properly. God expects you to rear faithful children (Deut. 6:1-2, Jer. 5:7); and if you live obediently, you should expect by his grace to rear faithful children (Deut. 7:9, Acts 2:39).

Only large quantities of time can provide the quality training your sons and daughters will need. You must therefore set your priorities and order your work so that they can observe your ways and learn from your example (Prov. 23:26, 1 Cor. 11:1). Share the gospel with your children by sharing your life with them. Work hard. Be pure and holy. Encourage and implore them to follow you in living worthily in God's kingdom (cf. 1 Thess. 2:8-12).

Preparation

Loving your parents and siblings is part of your preparation for marriage and child-rearing. Love your family by serving them. Look for other ways to serve in your church and community. That practice will teach you how to love your wife and children. Do not start bad habits of independence as a young man. They will be difficult for you to break when you have your own family.

Diligently study the Scriptures. Learn how a godly man exercises authority. Hide God's word in your heart so that you can keep your way pure (Ps. 119:9-16) and so that you can teach, reprove, correct, and train your wife and children in righteousness (2 Tim. 3:16).

Set goals for yourself and your future family. Figure out where you want to go and how you plan to get there. Do not ask a woman to follow you if you do not know where you are going.

Choose your occupation wisely. God provides our daily bread, but he expects us to work for it (Gen. 2:15, 2 Thess. 3:10). Therefore you need to do some sort of honest, profitable work, trusting God to provide for you and your family. Seriously consider operating your own free enterprise (1 Cor. 7:21, 1 Thess. 4:11-12). Such an arrangement gives you fuller control over how and where you work, and it allows you to interact more with your wife and children.

Learn to manage money. The central lesson is to live within your means. Follow Paul's simple words to owe nothing to anyone except love (Rom. 13:8). Debt enslaves you, it robs you of your freedom to give, and it will be a heavy burden on your family. If you are ever desperately in need of food and clothing, seek help from a brother in Christ. Otherwise, stay out of debt.

Do not expect your wife to bring home a paycheck. Her diligent and frugal work at home can save you money, and she may be able to sell some of the work of her hands; but if God blesses you with children, she will have plenty to occupy her time. If God blesses you with many children, you will have many hands to contribute to the family income. Choosing work in which your children can assist you will bless your family in many ways.

Do not be one of those young men who attracts attention to himself by his boisterous behavior or his unceasing jokes, often created at the expense of others. Be kind and friendly always, and be funny when appropriate. Distinguish yourself by your good deeds. Honor your father and mother. Develop your character. Pursue noble pursuits (1 Tim. 6:11).

A Wife's Roles

Submitting to Her Husband

Sarah obeyed Abraham, calling him lord, and women today can follow her example in doing right (1 Pet. 3:6). Though a wife should naturally and appropriately love her husband (Tit. 2:4, Eze. 16:45), the emphasis in Scripture is on her submission to her husband.

Male headship extends back to creation (1 Cor. 11:9, 1 Tim. 2:12-13), but Eve's sin confirmed the need for the wife's submission to her husband (Gen. 3:16, 1 Tim. 2:12-14). Since in Christ there is neither male nor female (Gal. 3:26-29), the believing wife of a believing husband is a fellow heir of the grace of life (1 Pet. 3:7). This does not mean that husbands and wives have identical roles or responsibilities.

Many men find that talking about wives submitting is easier than talking about husbands leading. If more men were good leaders, however, more women would be happy followers. Wives are instructed to be subject to their husbands (Eph. 5:22; cf. Eph. 5:33, Col. 3:18, Tit 2:5, 1 Pet 3:1-6), but as we noted above, the godly husband will not use his authority to lord it over his wife (Luke 22:25-26). Rather, he will love her as Christ loves the church, and she should gladly submit to him as the church submits to Christ. Though the husband carries the leadership responsibility, he should seek to know and to honor his wife's perspective.

A wife should express her internal submission by dressing and behaving modestly. She should not wear too little clothing (Eze. 16:8, 1 Cor. 12:23), but neither should she wear too much clothing and draw improper attention to herself by her appearance (1 Tim. 2:9). She should also avoid coming across as a talkative busybody (1 Tim. 5:13). Rather, the godly woman should exhibit chastity and respect (1 Pet. 3:2), distinguishing herself for God's glory by her good deeds (1 Tim. 2:10).

Helping Her Husband

The Lord decided that Adam needed a suitable helper, so he made Eve (Gen. 2:18, cf. 1 Cor. 11:9). God calls the wife to help her husband be fruitful and multiply, work diligently, and spread the gospel (Gen. 1:28, Acts 18:26). She should gladly honor God with her body by bearing children, by assisting her husband in his work, and by accompanying him in discipling the nations.

She should not be like Job's wife, who tried to get him to curse God (Job 2:9), or like Jezebel, who incited Ahab to do evil (1 Kin. 21:25). Neither should she nag or be contentious (Prov. 19:13, 21:9, 27:15-16). Rather the faithful wife will be a husband-lover (Tit. 2:4), giving him the encouragement, support, and intimacy that he needs (1 Cor. 7:2-5). An excellent wife makes a beautiful crown for her husband (Prov. 12:4). Her husband's heart trusts her, because she does him good and not evil (Prov. 31:11-12).

Managing Her Home

Paul calls the wife a "homeworker" or "homekeeper" in Titus 2:5 and literally a "homemaster" in 1 Timothy 5:14. Nearly every woman works somewhere doing something. People debate about what work she does, where she does it, and why she does it.

Do you want a career for personal satisfaction or to obtain wealth, or do you want to work for the good of your family like the woman in Proverbs 31? I want an industrious and frugal wife, but frankly I want her to work for me, and not for another man (Job 31:10). Employment is a form of servanthood, and my wife does not need to try to serve two "masters," her boss and me.

I expect my wife to do much of her work in and around our home, and I intend to spend much of my time there, too. I also hope that my mother and her mother and other older women in our church will do their job of assisting and training my wife as she continues to mature as a daughter of the Lord (Tit. 2:4-5).

Mothering Her Children

Bearing and training children is a good thing. Otherwise, Psalm 113:9 would not make any sense when it praises the Lord for turning the barren woman into a joyful mother. If children were such a terrible burden, then

I suppose barren women would be the happiest women in the world!

What "job" could match the benefits and blessings of motherhood? Instead of pushing papers in an office, you can be a teacher, nurse, interior decorator, and chef — all in the comfort of your own home! As a mother, you can help your husband rear your children in the nurture and admonition of the Lord. You can manage your home in such a way that its peaceful environment encourages the development of godly character. You can open your mouth in wisdom and let the teaching of kindness be on your tongue (Prov. 31:26).

Paul said that women shall be saved through childbearing, if they continue in faith, love, and holiness, with self-control (1 Tim. 2:15). The children of the noble wife arise and bless her, and her husband praises her excellent deeds (Prov. 31:28-29). Mothering children is a beautiful work (1 Tim. 5:10).

Preparation

Loving your parents and siblings is part of your preparation for marriage and child-rearing. Love your family by serving them. Look for other ways to serve in your church and community under your father's authority. That practice will teach you how to love your husband and children. Do not start bad habits of independence as a young woman. They will be difficult for you to break when you have your own family.

Diligently study the Scriptures. Learn how a godly woman conducts and presents herself. Hide God's word in your heart so that you can keep your way pure (Ps. 119:9-16) and so that you can teach, reprove, correct, and train your children in righteousness (2 Tim. 3:16).

Cultivate the skills you will need as the manager of your home. Develop frugal habits that will properly use your family's income. Take care of your body so that you will be prepared to bear and nourish children.

Both Rebekah and Rachel were working in their families when suitors came for them (Gen. 24:15-20, 29:9), and the law talks about an unmarried woman being in her father's house in her youth (Num. 30:3). Your father is your spiritual leader and protector now. Continuing to learn and to develop your skills under his loving care at home is a valuable blessing.

Do not be one of those young women who draws attention to herself through her immodest dress and behavior. The adulterous woman was boisterous and stubborn, and her feet did not remain at home (Prov. 7:11). A godly man will not want a woman who follows the latest improper fashions and fads. Honor your father and mother. Develop your character. Adorn your hidden person with a gentle and quiet spirit, which is precious in God's sight (1 Pet. 3:3-4).

Waiting

Guarding Your Heart

The springs of life flow from your heart, so you must watch it diligently (Prov. 4:23). The Old Testament tells how Absalom stole away the hearts of the people from his father, King David (2 Sam. 15:1-6). In the same way, numerous influences today seduce young men and women to give away their hearts to other people, even to glorified caricatures of people, in inappropriate ways and at inappropriate times.

This devotion can be romantic or non-romantic, depending on whether it is given to a movie star, a model, an athlete, a musician, or a boyfriend or girlfriend. We must pay careful attention to where we place our affections, and even where we direct our eyes.

Admiration is not wrong, but allowing that admiration to change into lust is. Job made a covenant with his eyes to help him avoid looking improperly at a virgin (Job 31:1). Jesus said that looking with lust shows adultery in the heart (Matt. 5:28).

The tenth commandment includes this injunction: You shall not covet your neighbor's wife (Ex. 20:17). Until you marry, you do not have a claim on the romantic affections of another person. If a young man develops a romantic relationship with a young woman outside of marriage, then he is essentially defrauding her father, her future husband, and his future wife (1 Thess. 4:3-7). He covets something that does not belong to him, and he tries to get it without making a commitment.

Flirting is wrong because it is a temptation to lust or to commit immorality. Flirting sends confusing signals, and if you do not stay away from flirts, you may easily be caught in their trap. Potiphar's wife cast her eyes at Joseph and tried to seduce him. He did not listen to her and tried to avoid her. When they were alone and she again tried to get his attention, he appropriately fled (Gen. 39:7-12).

The young man in Proverbs 7 was not so careful. He passed through the street near the corner of the adulterous woman, and she seduced him with her many persuasions and flattering lips (Prov. 7:6-23). The wise father counsels his son not to desire her beauty or let her catch him with her eyelids (Prov. 6:25).

Do not awaken love before the proper time. It will be worth the wait when God brings into your life the one person with whom you can share everything without fear or reservation.

Intimacy Outside of Marriage

Saints should have nothing to do with immorality, impurity, or greed (Eph. 5:3). The marriage bed should be undefiled because God will judge the fornicators and adulterers (Heb. 13:4). Besides the valuable benefits of saving intimacy for marriage, this warning should be a strong deterrent against not waiting.

Romantic touching has no place outside of marriage. God kept Abimelech from touching Sarah (Gen. 20:6). Boaz commanded his servants not to touch Ruth (Ruth 2:9). The proverb says that he who touches his neighbor's wife will not go unpunished (Prov. 6:29). Paul counseled that it is good for a man not to touch a woman (1 Cor. 7:1).

This general principle does not preclude all physical contact between unmarried men and women. For example, when the Lord used Peter to raise Dorcas from death, Peter gave her his hand and raised her up (Acts 9:41). The problem is romantic contact. If you would not do something with another man's wife in his presence, then do not do it with anyone besides your wife.

After I marry, I do not want another man to hold my wife's hand, kiss her, or otherwise touch her romantically. Nor do I want another man to touch my wife romantically before I marry her! Turning that thought around, I assume that other men do not want me to touch their wives romantically. I only want such contact with my wife anyway. Paul told Timothy to treat the young women as sisters, with complete purity (1 Tim. 5:2).

Physical intimacy does not help a boy and girl get to know each other better. It only fulfills their desires temporarily, and it distracts them from what they should be thinking about before marriage — the character and conduct of the other person. The marriage covenant gives a man and a woman the freedom to enjoy each other, and they should save their expressions of love for each other (Prov. 5:15-19).

Young men, do not seek to be alone with a woman besides your wife. Diligently avoid such situations. Young women, stay far away from men who want to be alone with you. Even if you are convinced that you would not "do anything," the appearance is wrong, and temptation could trap one or both of you.

When it comes to immorality, being careful is better than being sorry. Joseph did not intend to be alone with Potiphar's wife, but he still had to flee from a dangerous situation. Paul instructed Timothy to flee youthful lusts and to pursue the things that last (2 Tim. 2:22). If you play with fire, you should expect to get burned (Prov. 6:27-29).

The Bride Belongs to the Bridegroom

Marriage is an exclusive relationship between one man and one woman. Abusing that honorable union outside covenantal bounds is morally wrong. Young man, do not covet your neighbor's wife before or after you marry (Ex. 20:17). Young woman, do your husband good and not evil all the days of your life (Prov. 31:12).

Suppose I went to my friend's house and asked to take his daughter out to dinner alone. That happens, although the father is not usually involved these days. Now suppose I went to my friend's house and asked to take his wife out to dinner alone. What do you think he would say? What is the difference between these two situations? Why does the latter seem more bizarre than the former?

Sure, his daughter is not married yet, but she probably will be married to someone besides me. Our society has decided that playing around with other people's emotions and bodies is okay before marriage. I suspect that is why playing around with other people's emotions and bodies is common after marriage.

The bride belongs to the bridegroom (John 3:29). In all of our male-female relationships, we need to act with holiness, thinking about the implications of our actions. We must take great care not to defraud someone, especially a brother or sister, of something that is irreplaceable — an undivided heart (1 Thess. 4:1-8).

Betrothal & Marriage

When you read the Biblical accounts of how marriages were formed, what stands out in your mind? Do they have something to teach us, or are they just old-fashioned stories with moral messages? What general principles can we combine with direct Scriptural teaching to develop an outline for how a young man should seek a wife?

Recent years have brought a number of books on this subject. Unmarried people have been encouraged to kiss dating goodbye, give dating a chance, and nearly everything in-between. I am not going to lay out a rigid system for perfect marriage manufacture, but I will take the risk of offering my observations.

Some things we should consciously do, and others we should consciously avoid. However, I do not think the process should be as complicated as some people make it. As with many things in life, we have a set of instructions and principles given by God. He provides success when we follow him obediently.

Relationship With Parents Before Marriage

What sort of relationship do young people in the Biblical accounts have with their parents? Perhaps you have noticed that nearly all of them were living with their parents until the time they married. Jacob did leave home to find a wife, but he left with Isaac's blessing and instruction. Boaz was apparently older and living on his own. However, the Biblical pattern appears simply to be that a man shall leave his parents and cleave to his wife (Gen. 2:24).

As we saw before, the Biblical command to honor your father and mother does not just apply to little children. It applies to young people who are considering marriage. If you are still living with your parents, then be thankful that they are close by to help guide and oversee your preparation for marriage. If you are not living with your parents, then you need to maintain contact with them and seek their direction. You will also need other mature believers around you to hold you accountable.

Age at Marriage

The Bible does not give many specifics on when people married. Isaac and Esau were both forty when they married (Gen. 25:20, 26:34). Pharaoh gave Joseph a wife when he was thirty (Gen. 41:45). Abraham was ten years older than Sarah (Gen. 17:17). Based on the numbers given in 2 Chronicles, some of the kings of Judah apparently married in their teens.

Frequently the Scriptures talk about marriage "in one's youth." A husband should rejoice in the wife of his youth (Prov. 5:18). The adulteress in Proverbs 2:17 leaves the companion of her youth. God commanded that no one should deal treacherously against the wife of his youth (Mal. 2:15). Psalm 127:3-4 talks about the blessing of the children of one's youth.

Young people should not rush into marriage, nor should parents push them into it. Neither should young people who are prepared for marriage feel compelled to wait for an imaginary age threshold. Postponing marriage without due cause can bring unnecessary temptation (1 Cor. 7:2) and create an unnatural "singles" mentality. Proper training and wise counsel can help men and women form strong marriages whenever they are ready.

The Father's Authority

A father should prepare his sons and his daughters for marriage and should help them find an appropriate mate. Because the father has responsibility for the spiritual well-being of his children, he has the right to keep his children from marrying in violation of Biblical teaching.

On the other hand, a loving father will not force his child to marry someone against his or her will. Everyone seemed convinced that Rebekah should become Isaac's wife, but they still asked her if she would go with Abraham's servant (Gen. 24:58). She consented and went. We are not told whether Isaac was given a similar choice, but he does not seem to have minded his father's choice!

The Father's Authority Over His Sons

Abraham took the lead in getting a wife for Isaac (Gen. 24). Judah took a wife for his son Er (Gen. 38:6). The judge Ibzan took wives for his thirty sons (Judg. 12:9). King Rehoboam sought many wives for his sons (2 Chr. 11:23).

God warned the Israelites against choosing pagan women to marry their sons (Ex. 34:13-16).

The priest Eli knew the sins that his sons were committing. They brought a curse on themselves, and Eli did not properly restrain them. God judged him for his carelessness (1 Sam. 2:22). A father may direct his son in choosing a proper wife, but this should be a two-sided effort. A good son will welcome his father's guidance, and a good father will give it wisely. I do not want to marry someone my parents do not like, and they do not want me to marry someone I do not like!

Scripture does contain examples of men choosing wives for themselves, without their father's direct supervision. Several of these were older men who had established households. After Sarah died, when he was about 140 years old, Abraham took another wife for himself (Gen. 25:1). Solomon took the throne of Israel after his father David's death, and he literally "made himself" Pharaoh's son-in-law (1 Kin. 3:1). Boaz was an older man (Ruth 3:10) with fields and servants when he married Ruth.

Other examples of men choosing wives without parental guidance are negative. For instance, Esau, at age forty, married Judith and Basemath, which brought grief to his parents Isaac and Rebekah (Gen. 26:34-35). Judah left his brothers and took the daughter of a Canaanite as his wife. You can read about the fruit of that union in Genesis 38. Young men who rush into marriage without parental blessing are asking for trouble.

Both the headstrong Samson and the pagan Shechem spoke to their fathers about getting the girls they liked as wives (Judg. 14:2; Gen. 34:4). A righteous young man should gladly seek his father's counsel as he considers marriage. His parents may identify a good match for him, or he may bring a certain girl to their attention, but if everyone is working toward the same goal (a healthy marriage) with the same motive (God's glory), then collaboration can only be beneficial.

Young men, listen to your father and mother and do not marry a young woman of whom they disapprove. You will bring trouble on yourself and scar your relationship with your parents. Let their years of wisdom guide you in your selection process.

The Father's Authority Over His Daughters

The Scriptures assume that a young woman will be under the real authority and protection of her father until she marries. When he met her, Abraham's servant assumed that Rebekah was still living with her father (Gen. 24:23). The widowed or divorced daughter of a priest could return to her father's house as in her youth (Lev. 22:13). When Boaz saw Ruth in his field, he assumed that she was under someone's care (Ruth 2:5).

Some fathers abuse their authority, and others neglect their protective responsibilities. Both Lot and the man in Gibeah offered their virgin daughters to the perverted mobs at their doors (Gen. 19:8, Judg. 19:24). Jacob's daughter Dinah was violated while she was out visiting the daughters of the land (Gen. 34:1-2). Jacob let Dinah go out among the pagans, apparently alone. Young women need protection (cf. Deut. 22:27).

These examples of corruption should not turn us away from the proper perspective. They should encourage us to follow it! Fathers, take your position seriously. Protect your daughter from young men who want to be alone with her (2 Sam. 13:6-14).

If an improper suitor approaches you concerning your daughter, you should refuse his petition without burdening your daughter. If you let him get close to her, he might steal her heart. Even in that case, even if they have lain together, you still have the right and responsibility to refuse to give her to a bad husband (Ex. 22:16-17). Guard her with a godly jealousy, that you may present her to one husband as a pure virgin (2 Cor. 11:2-3).

Young women, submit to your father's protection. Do not look for romance behind his back. Do not give your heart to a man who attempts to draw it to himself before the proper time. Accept your father's decision if he turns away a potential husband without fearing that you will never find someone else. Rest in his desire to do you good, and wait for him to present a godly suitor to you for consideration.

A Different Approach

I realize that details will vary for each couple because of multiple factors, so understand again that I am not laying out a marriage-making mold. This plan may even change for me, but I want to bring together the various concepts I have been sharing so far. You will see how I expect them to work in real life.

For good reasons of his own choosing, God may not give me a wife. He may have another avenue of service prepared for me, and I will gladly serve him unmarried in that case. If the Lord wills, I do intend to marry, and the following words assume that coming event.

The goal of the marriage formation process is not to have fun. It is not to develop social skills. It is not to bind children into unhappily arranged marriages. The goal of the marriage formation process is to bring a faithful man and a faithful woman into a blessed union by the arrangement of God working through wise parents and other counselors.

I do not have a convenient term for this process. I gave up "courtship" because it has acquired too much baggage. "Betrothal" refers to the period immediately preceding marriage when the two parties have committed to their union but have not yet come together. The "waiting and looking" stage seems to be a natural part of life during which young men and women treat each other with respect, show honor to their parents, and prepare themselves to handle the responsibilities of adulthood.

My Plan

Trusting God to provide our daily bread, I am establishing myself to be able to feed and clothe a wife and children properly. I plan to have a suitable dwelling prepared for my wife by the time we marry. I continue to study the Scriptures in regard to family life and to set goals for my family.

As I prepare for marriage, my parents and I are looking for a young woman to be my wife. We spend time with other families by visiting and receiving visitors. We interact with those in our church and in other churches in our area. We maintain contact with friends in other parts of the country. If a particular girl attracts my attention, I can subtly learn more about her by observing her behavior, by talking with her family members and friends, and by interacting with her in group activities.

Correspondence may seem like a good way for me to get to know a young woman without dating, but sustained private communication has a serious drawback that needs consideration. Even if our parents supervised our exchanges, we would be spending much personal time together in our thoughts. We would quickly run out of suitable topics of discussion in our letters, and our thoughts would readily turn to issues that are too serious or too sensitive for platonic dialogue. Dating by correspondence can cause problems, too.

My parents and I will only consider a faithful disciple of Jesus Christ. We also want a girl who has similar views on religious and other significant matters. Marriage is enough of a challenge without asking for conflict from the beginning. In addition we are looking for a young woman ready and willing to assume the duties of wife and mother. My wife may come from a far away place, but I expect her to come from one of the families we know and love, a girl with whom we have spent time in various situations.

When we identify a potential wife, then we (or I with my parents' blessing) can talk to her father concerning the match. I want and expect him to interrogate me thoroughly concerning my beliefs, experiences, and plans. He should feel confident that I am devoted to the Lord, that I have shown industry and responsibility, and that I am prepared to support a wife and children. We can also work out questions about living location, church fellowship, and such practical matters that are important to one family or the other.

He may rightly consult with those who know me, and he may ask me to participate with him in some study or activity. If he and his wife believe that I would be a good husband for their daughter, then I trust they will seek her consent. When all parties involved are agreed, she and I will become betrothed.

From the Scriptures, I understand betrothal to be the special period just before a man and woman come together in marriage. They are committed to each other, but they do not yet live together (Matt. 1:18,19). Under the continued oversight of our parents, I expect our emotional attachment to flourish, yet still without physical expression. Since we are committed to each other, we can freely share hopes and dreams and look forward to the future, trusting together in the good God who brought us to that point.

As part of the marriage arrangements, my wife's father may rightly ask me to pay a bride price (Gen. 34:12, Ex 22:17, 1 Sam. 18:25). This would be a signification of my serious commitment and a confirmation of my ability to support his daughter.

Depending on the circumstances, the betrothal period may last a few weeks or a few months. When the time comes for the celebration of our union, we will enjoy a wonderful wedding to confirm our covenant union before God (Prov. 2:17, Eze. 16:8, Mal. 2:14). My bride will properly adorn herself (Rev. 21:2), I will rejoice over her (Isa. 62:5), and our family and friends will rejoice with us (John 3:29). The Scriptures certainly authorize extended feasting and celebration in honor of a wedding.

Marriage involves leaving father and mother, but it does not require that sons and daughters move away from their parents. I would be glad for my wife and me to live near our parents, continuing to learn from them, allowing our children to know them well, and growing with them as brothers and sisters in the Lord.

We must be careful not to be exclusive toward others, but extended family ties are good. Families do not have to splinter and segregate. Working together we can accomplish great things for God's kingdom. If our parents require care as they age, then my wife and I, by God's grace, will put our religion into practice by caring for them in our home (1 Tim. 5:4).

Celebrating the first year of our marriage with a precious baby in our arms would be the best anniversary present we could share. I pray that God would make our union fruitful and give us many arrows, weapons of righteousness that we can sharpen for his service. However many children he gives us, we will seek to bring them up in his nurture and admonition, according to his commands.

For God's glory we will seek to illustrate the union of Christ and the church, to rear godly children for his service, to exercise dominion over the earth, and to spread the gospel by teaching and discipling others. That is how we can live happily ever after and enjoy what God joins together.

Chapter 11

Receiving Children for God's Glory

Have you ever been driving along and realized you were headed in the wrong direction? Was it on a limited-access highway? Finding a place to turn around and then backtracking is frustrating and tiring. Starting in the right direction is much easier than changing course later!

I want to develop a Biblical attitude about children now, before I am married, because I want to start in the right direction when I do marry. I want to encourage my brothers and sisters in the Lord to think about their attitude toward little ones. I want to challenge myself, and I am willing to challenge popular opinion. I want to be an articulate advocate for the truth, even as a young man.

And I am looking for a wife who wants to receive and rear many children for God's glory.

Once when we had traveled to West Tennessee on business, we were waiting at a fast food restaurant to meet a relative. A white minivan from the Midwest pulled into the parking lot, and a young couple got out. The woman looked quite young, and the man had a long ponytail. A couple of children hopped out after them. Just your average family, right? Well, children three, four, and five hopped out after the others, and they walked into the restaurant together!

Not too long ago, families with more than one or two children were much more common than they are today. Now families with three children are seen as pushing the limits of propriety. Going beyond that is unthinkable for many. I heard a father of two ask a mother of five if her quiver was full yet. Not only are such questions rude; they betray a disregard for the blessing of the womb. What should our attitude be?

The Bible warns us against following the crowd, so we need to keep our eyes and ears and minds open. The Bible must be the ultimate standard by which we examine our beliefs. What does the Bible say about children? The Bible tells us that children are a blessing, that God controls the womb, and that we should be fruitful and multiply.

Children Are a Blessing

Many parents like to quote Psalm 127, even those who are not convinced of the need to multiply fruitfully. It is a lovely and touching reminder that children are a gift. As any new parent knows, children are valuable just because of who they are. Sarah was delighted at the arrival of her Isaac (Gen. 18:12, 21:6-7), and Jesus said that the birth of a child brings joy (John 16:21). Children are precious because God made them, and they bring joy to parents who love and train them properly (Prov. 29:17).

Children are also valuable because they can contribute to the family prosperity. Large families are considered blessed in Scripture (Ruth 4:11-12, 1 Chr. 26:4-8, Ps. 128), and we see numerous examples of children working responsibly with and under their fathers: Noah's sons (Gen. 6-9), Rebekah (Gen. 24), Gideon (Judg. 6:11), David (1 Samuel 16:14-19), and evidently Jesus himself (Matt. 13:55 and Mark 6:3). Children are listed in Leviticus 26 and Deuteronomy 28 as a blessing of obedience right along with good weather, healthy crops, and productive animals.

When children grow up well, they bring honor to their parents. The end of Psalm 127 compares children to arrows in the hands of a warrior. They are trained and ready to speak with their enemies in the gate. Grown children can also take care of Dad and Mom when necessary (1 Tim. 5:4), and they can produce grandchildren (Ps. 128:6, Prov. 17:6)!

God Controls the Womb

God controls the conception, development, and birth of children. He has usually given conception to younger women who lie with a man at certain times when neither of them seeks to prevent it. However, he who gave conception to the virgin is able to work differently in different cases according to his will.

Ruth 4:13 literally says that God gave Ruth conception. Several passages speak of the Lord opening and closing the womb (Gen. 20:17,18; 29:31; 30:22; 1 Sam. 1:5), and other passages clearly show his control (e.g., Gen. 21:1,2; 30:17; 1 Sam. 2:21). The ancients rightly believed that God gave children (e.g., Gen. 4:1, 16:2, 30:2). He normally exercises His supernatural power through the natural means He has created (cf. Ruth 4:13, 1 Sam. 1:19), but that does not negate his creative authority.

Job knew that God fashioned us in the womb (Job 31:15), and the Psalmist acknowledged God as his maker (Psalm 119:73). The Lord told the Israelites that he, the maker of all things, was the one who formed them from the womb (Isa. 44:24). God knew Jeremiah even before he formed him in the womb (Jer. 1:5). David's beautiful passage in Psalm 139:13-16 praises God for how he fearfully and wonderfully knits together a baby's inward parts in the mother's womb. God's authority even extends over "birth defects." He told Moses that he, the Lord, makes men dumb or deaf or seeing or blind (Ex. 4:11). Physical problems may or may not be directly related to sin, but in all of them, God is working for his glory and honor (John 9:2-3).

Be Fruitful and Multiply

The first recorded command given to male and female was to be fruitful and multiply, to fill the earth and subdue it (Gen. 1:28). Twice after the flood God commanded Noah and his sons to "be fruitful and multiply" (Gen. 9:1,7), and he repeated the command to Jacob (Gen. 35:11). When the Jews were exiles in Babylon, they were facing tough times. Surely that would have been a good time to control their procreation. No! God instructed them to marry, have children, and marry off their children so that they would multiply there and not decrease (Jer. 29:6). Paul taught Timothy that younger widows should marry, bear children, keep house, and give the enemy no occasion for reproach (1 Tim. 5:14).

Since God is the one who gives children, a husband and wife who earnestly want children may remain childless. In that case, they can minister to children in other ways, perhaps by adopting children. In his wisdom and providence, God tells us to do that which he enables us to do. He asks husbands and wives to do their part, but they cannot honestly take credit for making plants grow, for making businesses succeed, or even for making babies. Duty is ours. Results are God's!

Being Pro-Life

We live in a culture that does not like children. Many young couples say, "Maybe later," in regards to bearing children, and after they have had one or two they say, "That's enough!" Hundreds of thousands of children are killed in the womb every year, and babies are left to die in hospital closets and garbage cans. America was rightly sorrowful when some 3,000 people died on September 11, 2001. Why is America not sorrowful when, on average, 3,000 children are killed in the womb every day? Those children who manage to survive the womb are often abused through lack of discipline, passed from caregiver to caregiver, drugged into submission, and eventually left unprepared to fend for themselves.

Pagan behavior should not surprise us in a country that has abandoned God's moral code. Child abuse and sacrifice go back centuries. What does surprise and disturb me is the fact that while many believers are "anti-death," they are not truly "pro-life." They do not like people to kill unwanted children, but they do not want any more children for themselves. People who are blessed with several children make them nervous.

At a church picnic of all places, I heard a man say, "I wouldn't take a million dollars for my son, but I wouldn't give five dollars for another one!" You, too, have probably heard jokes about big families and lamentations about the "burden" of children. Have you ever heard a sermon contradicting popular opinion on reproduction? Have you heard much thanksgiving for the true blessing of children among your friends and fellow believers?

Some groups like the Old Order Amish still average 6 or more children per family, but many American churches follow the cultural trends with the appropriate 1.8 children per family. I do not attribute this state of affairs to a general decline in fertility; instead, we have seen a general decline in receptivity to the blessing of children.

We know of a man and woman who both had polio and were confined to wheelchairs from childhood. They married, had five children, and served as missionaries in France and England. One of their daughters and her husband (who are good friends of our family) are now serving as missionaries in Germany. They have six children and are expecting number seven! One of the original couple's sons and his wife have been missionaries in England and have adopted children from Africa. Even couples who have special challenges can give children a blessed home in which to grow up.

Throughout history God's people have desired children. They have considered children a blessing, and more children meant greater blessing. Today the church has largely come to believe that children are a burden, and that even one or two may be too expensive, too challenging, or too troublesome. Until the church renews a positive attitude toward children and accepts other basic Biblical teachings, I fear that our influence in the world will continue to suffer. Let us be pro-life!

Practical Benefits

Bringing up children requires time and discipline from parents. It requires extra resources, too. The more children you have, however, the more you can spread around the responsibilities and have additional hands contributing to the family supply of resources. What practical benefits come with having many children and rearing them well?

1. You can enjoy them. Since one well-trained child is a delight to the soul (Prov. 29:17), think how much delight ten would bring!

2. You can have more grandchildren. Imagine how many grandchildren and great-grandchildren could be placed on your knee if your quiver is full (Gen. 50:23).

3. You can have more people to help you in your work. Obed-Edom was a gatekeeper among the priestly families. He had eight sons and many descendants who were strong and valiant. The text says that God had indeed blessed him (2 Chr. 26:4-8).

4. You can contribute to the success of your community. A large population is a glory for the king (Prov. 14:28), and large godly families can promote the welfare of even pagan cities (Jer. 29:6-7).

5. You can start your own country (Gen. 35:11). Okay, maybe I am stretching this one a bit. However, your large family of multiple generations can be a vibrant community in its own right.

6. You can spread good news. Philip the evangelist had four daughters who were prophetesses (Acts 21:8-9).

7. You can know at the end of your life that you invested yourself in something worthwhile (Gen. 18:19, 1 Tim. 5:10).

Parenting

I am assuming that you will want to train properly any children you produce. You must help them to know and serve the Lord, to be wise and responsible and compassionate. I am not arguing simply that we should receive more children. I am arguing that we should receive more children for God's glory. Doing that means making conscious decisions and sacrifices.

Neither quality time nor quantity time is good enough on its own. My children will need large quantities of quality time with my wife and me. We must follow the same principles we expect our children to follow. If they do not see through hypocrisy right away, they will at least be disappointed later on. We must be careful that the example we set for them is a good one.

Children are like clay tablets slowly hardening in the sun. Early and often we must teach them God's message, trusting God's spirit to mold and mend their hearts. We cannot wait until they grow up and then try chiseling truth into their hardened hearts. To help our children develop self-control, we must get them started on the right track. Training to instill right behavior and correction to remove wrong behavior go hand in hand.

Besides the most important task of preparing them for eternity, we must also equip them with the knowledge and skills they need to serve the Lord on earth. By training them at home, we can give them a quality education and help them be ready to serve God by establishing godly households of their own.

Conclusion

Since I must be ready to explain to my future father-in-law my attitude toward children, I have developed these convictions that I plan to carry into marriage. I trust that my future wife will understand and agree with me before we are betrothed. I did not arrive at this understanding overnight, and I know many of the people around me have grown up in an anti-child environment.

My peers are marrying, and I have encouraged a few of those close to me to welcome children as a blessing from the beginning. I have not had an overwhelming response so far. Maybe they will listen to me after I lead by example, but I am sorry that they are missing the blessing now. Young married people who think that children will ruin their newlywed bliss have the wrong idea about marriage. As long as we expect children to be a pain in the neck, we should not be surprised when they are!

If you are unmarried like me, evaluate your attitude toward children long before you make or accept an offer for marriage. Look for someone who shares your views. We men need to be ready to love, lead, train, protect, and supply a house full of little ones. You women need to be ready to love, nurture, and help them grow up in the Lord.

If you are still unsure whether or not you are ready and willing to handle a new child, please do not use birth control pills. They interfere with a woman's reproductive organs in such a way that they can contribute to the death of a newly-conceived baby. The intra-uterine device (IUD) has a similar problem. Since other contraceptive methods have their own drawbacks, you may decide that having another child is not so bad!

God blesses different families in different ways, so I am not suggesting that every couple must produce a specified quota of children. I estimate that while the Israelites were in Egypt before the exodus, God blessed them with about 10 children per family. I would be glad if God blessed my wife and me so richly!

I need to live out my convictions happily and graciously and teach my children to be thoroughly pro-life by my attitude and action. I do not want people to beget children that they do not want. I do want my brothers and sisters to desire children and to accept them gladly from the Lord so that our families will expand their influence in the world, our churches will grow in strength and in number, and God will be glorified by the fruitful multiplication that he provides!

Chapter 12

Civic Duties

In warning the Philippians not to set their minds on earthly things, Paul properly reminded them that our citizenship is in heaven (Phil. 3:20). Every disciple in every nation shares that high calling, regardless of his local political situation.

We can give too much attention to political matters, and we can put too much trust in the power of government to do good, but Paul set us the example of using his Roman citizenship to advantage in God's service. He understood Roman law and custom; and when the opportunity arose, Paul appealed his case to the highest human authority: Caesar himself (Acts 21-28). The Lord wanted Paul to be a witness in Rome, and he used the Roman political system to accomplish that (Acts 23:11).

On occasion we may be forced to choose obedience to God rather than to government, but in general our civic duties will be a complementary part of our spiritual duties. How can we properly render to Caesar what is Caesar's and to God what is God's?

We must pray. We must perform good deeds. We can also contribute to the health of our nation by studying history and current events, by educating others, by seeing government in action, by examining candidates and voting, and by running for office. Let us explore these in more detail.

Prayer

Our first duty as citizens is to pray. Paul directly enjoins this in his first letter to Timothy (2:1-7). He calls for requests, prayers, intercessions, and thanksgivings for all men, including kings and those in authority. The desired result is that we may lead quiet and peaceable lives in all godliness and seriousness. This, in turn, contributes to the spread of the gospel. The Lord gave a similar instruction to the Jewish exiles in Babylon. In a letter sent through Jeremiah, God told the Jews to pray for the city they were in. If it had peace, then they would have peace (Jer. 29:7).

We also see examples of prayer when God's people had dealings with the civil authorities. Esther asked the Jews to fast before she went in to the king (Est. 4:16). Daniel offered a quick prayer while he was talking with the king (Neh. 2:4). King Darius recognized God's power and wanted the Jews to pray for him and his sons (Ezra 6:10). Even hard-hearted Pharaoh asked Moses to pray for him (Ex. 8:28, 12:32). The early disciples prayed together when Peter and John were released (Acts 4:24-31) and when Peter was in prison (Acts 12:5).

We are supposed to pray all the time about everything, which must include the issues of righteousness, justice, and peace that we face in the civil sphere. The energetic prayers of righteous people can have great positive effect in our cities and countries.

Good Deeds

Simply mouthing words is not what prayer is about. God expects us to follow up our prayers with action. Often he uses us as the answers to our own prayers by enabling us to meet the needs and right the wrongs we see. Being a good citizen does not prove faithfulness to God, but every disciple of Christ should be a good citizen.

In Philippians 1:27, Paul exhorts us literally to "behave as citizens" in a manner worthy of the gospel. Likewise the passage in Jeremiah does not just command prayer. God told the Jews to seek the peace of the city where he sent them (Jer. 29:7). We are the light of the world and a city on a hill. The good example of our lives is a seasoning influence on the society around us.

We also show our righteousness through obedience to the law of the land. Among people who try to cut corners and push limits, we can exhibit honesty and self-control. The state does not deserve our worship, but it does deserve our respect. The will of God includes submission to human authorities, by which we can put to silence the ignorance of foolish men. We are free men, but we are bondslaves of God (1 Pet. 2:13-17).

My Suggestions

Prayer and good deeds are what God clearly requires of us in the civil sphere. Some argue that this should be the extent of our political involvement. They maintain that since we are aliens and strangers who belong to a spiritual kingdom, we should not get mixed up in the affairs of earthly kingdoms. This perspective has attractive features, and it is perhaps an understandable reaction to abuses of political power. By no means should we trust in princes instead of the Lord.

However, the Lord turns the heart of the king (Prov. 21:1), and he may choose to use us as instruments to that end. Daniel's faithfulness to King Darius led Darius to issue a decree instructing his subjects to fear and tremble before the God of Daniel (Dan. 6).

The Scriptures convince me that we should be attentive to and active in the political realm. Who can better make decisions that affect the lives and liberty of thousands or millions of people — a faithful servant of God or a selfish, power-seeking humanist? If a pagan ruler put his faith in Jesus, would we want him to abdicate and turn his authority over to another pagan?

Instead of abandoning the political process, we should learn how we can serve God effectively as citizens and as civil magistrates. Here are five ideas for your consideration.

1) Study history and current events.

In Acts chapter 7, Stephen has been dragged to the Sanhedrin, the high council of Jewish leaders. He is accused of speaking against the temple and the law. With his face like the face of an angel, Stephen commences an account of the history of the Hebrew nation from Abraham to Solomon. He denounces the rulers and declares that they are the ones who have not kept the law. Stephen's detailed knowledge of history allows him to make a reasoned defense before the council.

In response to this rousing speech, the challenged audience did not welcome Stephen as a member of their circle. He did not get a proverbial seat at the political table. He was promptly taken out and stoned to death. Standing up for what is right will not necessarily win political friends and influence political people. Often it will not. We should not go along to get along politically. Instead, we should be willing to speak the truth in love.

Jesus in Luke 13:1-5 illustrates the value of knowing current events by using two tragic events to make a spiritual point about repentance. In our media-saturated age, we are exposed to much so-called news, which is largely a collection of sensational and unrelated tidbits. We can hear the same stories and the same commentary over and over through TV, radio, newspapers, magazines, and the Internet. Simply knowing the news is not the point. We must look for the how and the why behind current events and recognize spiritual implications.

Like the sons of Issachar of old, we should understand the times and have knowledge about what our nation should do (1 Chr. 12:32). One valuable activity that many citizens neglect is reading and understanding the Constitution of the United States of America, the Declaration of Independence, and other important historical documents such as the Constitution of your state, the Federalist and Anti-Federalist papers, addresses by George Washington and other early leaders, and Supreme Court opinions (for example, the majority and minority opinions in *Roe v. Wade*).

If we do not know the foundational principles of our nation, and if we do not know how we have gotten where we are, then we will have trouble knowing how and where we should go from here. If we understand history and current events, then we will have an advantage in civil affairs. We can identify faulty arguments and proposals. We can recommend reasonable alternatives. We can speak confidently with wisdom, inviting others to consider the value of God's ways.

2) Educate others.

You can host a government study group using videos or books. You can contribute to organizations that promote good government. You can publish your own news source, such as my e-mail newsletter in which I offer commentary on current events and social issues. (You can subscribe by e-mailing me at john@notgrass.com.) These efforts might not convert multitudes to your position right away, but you can at least highlight the issues before us.

Educating others includes educating government officials. Since they represent us, they need to hear from us. Our contact with them, whether in writing or in person, should be respectful and well-mannered. Careless communication may do more harm than good. Officials who do not share our core values may be less attentive than those who do, but even those who disagree may be brought around on particular issues. In my state of Tennessee, a legislator proposed a bill allowing extra testing of non-public high school students. Homeschoolers flooded the capitol with contacts, and the representative withdrew his bill.

A dramatic event in the Bible had much greater implications than a plan for student testing. Haman had gotten the king of Persia to authorize the complete destruction of the Jewish people. The Jewish woman Esther was the queen, but even she did not have the right to approach the king's inner court without permission. Bracing herself to do her duty regardless of the consequences, she approached the king and found favor in his sight. Esther soon exposed Haman's plot and the Jews were enabled to resist and defeat their opponents.

We should use our various skills in various ways to educate others about the importance of following the truth.

3) See government in action.

After we moved to the district of a new state representative, I visited the state capitol and introduced myself to him. He asked if I was lobbying. (I guess most people who visit the capitol want something!) I had not come regarding a particular issue that day. I wanted to get a better feel for how the state legislature worked and to make contacts. I accompanied a woman who has been a volunteer lobbyist on family issues for many years. Through her many connections, I was able to meet several other legislators that day.

Starting on the local level may be easiest for you. City council and county commission meetings are not always highly dramatic, but you may be surprised at what comes up and how things are handled. By attending the meetings, you may be able to meet others in your community with similar interests. You can at least find out who takes political issues seriously enough to attend.

Seeing government in action will enlighten you. It will probably also disappoint you. All government officials are men and women with emotions and biases, strengths and struggles. Some of them have noble ideals and others do not give that impression. The more you get to know your representatives, the more you may be able to influence them for good.

4) Examine the candidates and vote.

When Moses was with the Israelites in the wilderness, his father-in-law Jethro offered counsel that deserves to be repeated. He advised Moses to select assistant judges to help him in his work: men who fear God, men of truth, and men who hate covetousness (Ex. 18:17-23).

It seems so simple. Who else would we pick? Alas, many people do not share this perspective. They would rather select a candidate who promises the most goodies or runs the best advertisements. Without thinking about the consequences, they vote for people who do not have the best interests of their city, state, or country in mind.

Your vote is a valuable commodity that belongs to you. It does not belong to the Constitution Party, the Democratic Party, the Green Party, the Libertarian Party, the Reform Party, the Republican Party, the Socialist Party, or any other group. It does not belong by default to any candidate.

If a candidate wants your vote, he must earn it by the way he conducts himself and his campaign, by the principles he espouses and embodies in office and out of office. We should not have to cajole and beg and threaten our legislators to support life, liberty, and the pursuit of righteousness. Rather we should put in office men who will do what is right out of principle.

Ask basic questions about the candidate. Does he believe that our rights and responsibilities come from government or from God? Does he believe that some lives are unworthy of respect or that every life is precious? Does he believe that morality is determined by polls or that God has given us instruction regarding right and wrong?

Investigate for yourself. Consider all your options. Do not trust the newspaper or the radio or the TV to give you the full story. Do not think that a candidate is worthy of your support simply because he belongs to a particular party. Do not waste your vote on someone who does not share your values and priorities. Do not vote against someone out of fear. Vote for someone with conviction. Vote your conscience. Even if your chosen candidate does not prevail in the end, you can be confident that your vote was well spent. The results of every election are in the hand of God. He asks us to do our duty.

5) Consider running for office.

Barnabas and Saul preached to Sergius Paulus, the intelligent proconsul on the island of Cyprus; and he believed (Acts 13:12). Paul sent greetings to the Romans from Erastus, who was a city official, evidently in Corinth (Rom. 16:23). When Paul was speaking before Festus, King Agrippa, Bernice, and other eminent personages, he responded to Agrippa's statement about making a Christian with the prayer that all those listening to him might become like him, except for his chains (Acts 26:29).

We should keep praying for our officials, even for those who oppose right principles. Maybe God will lead them to repentance and conversion! If you have trouble finding worthy candidates to support, consider running for office yourself. Godly officeholders can do great good.

I recommend this primarily for men. A lack of sufficient suitable male representatives reflects poorly on our gender. This preference is in no way a denigration of the capabilities or intelligence of women. It is a reflection of the way God made the world.

Examine your motives. You should not seek office so you can lord it over others or acquire wealth and glory. Examine your situation. If other responsibilities demand your attention now, then statesmanship may need to wait. Many an officeholder steps down so he can "spend more time with his family." Do not let anything, including politics, distract you from your most important duties to God, family, and church. However, if you see that service in the civil sphere is an appropriate use of your talents that complements your other efforts, give it a try!

Conclusion

God gave the Israelites some 613 commandments dealing with every area of life from family relationships to eating habits to criminal prosecution to religious practices. God's instructions were not too difficult or out of reach (Deut 30:11), but the people still fell short. What are we to do with today's modern legal codes containing thousands of complex statutes? We do not need many laws. The Lord summed up our responsibilities with the two great commandments to love him and to love our neighbor.

Since we do not always follow those basic rules, however, God has instituted human governments to praise those who do well and to punish those who do evil (Rom. 13:1-7). God uses pagan rulers to accomplish his purposes (Ex. 7:3-5, Isa. 45). He can use believers, too (Prov. 29:2). Government is not the savior of mankind. Government is a force that needs to be controlled carefully. Men who fear God are better equipped to handle that responsibility.

The cry of theocracy is often raised against those of us who seek to implement Biblical principles in civil government, but all governments are subservient to a higher power, either the god of this world or the God of the universe. God is already king by divine right. We can decide to acknowledge his authority now or later.

We can all pray. We can all do good deeds. You may not all do all of the other things I have discussed here, but you should use the opportunities available to you to seek the peace and prosperity of your community. I want people to live free and safe so that they can work for good by training their children, sharing with those in need, building healthy businesses, and enjoying the world God gave us.

Chapter 13

The Household of God

Since before the foundation of the world, the Author of Life has desired intimacy with the people made in his own image. He provided us with every physical blessing, but we rejected him in order to pursue our own desires. The Almighty has not remained silent, though. Speaking to us through prophets at many times and in various ways, and in these last days speaking to us in his Son, the Holy One has not abandoned us to the grave. Rather he has given us the opportunity to know him and to reign with him as his true children.

Knowing the Story

In the beginning, God created the heaven and the earth. At his command, light came into existence. God made an expanse between the waters and formed dry ground in the midst of the water on earth. He called vegetation out of the ground and set light-bearers in the expanse of the sky to mark seasons, days, and years. The water teemed with living creatures, and birds began their flights above the earth. The land produced all kinds of animals, and God saw that it was good.

Then God made *adam*, male and female he created them, and God saw that it was very good. He blessed them and told them to be fruitful and multiply, to fill the earth and subdue it. He gave them authority over the fish, birds, and land animals, and offered them a vegetarian diet. They were both naked, and they felt no shame. Shame arrived with disobedience.

By obeying God's simple commands, our first parents could have avoided the anguish that accompanies a knowledge of evil. They sinned when, encouraged by the serpent, they gave expression to the lust of the flesh, the lust of the eyes, and the pride of life (1 John 2:16). They tried to hide, but they could not escape from the Lord's presence. In righteous judgment, God pronounced punishment for everyone involved. He also stated that somewhere down the line, one of the woman's descendants would crush the serpent's head.

Humanity began life outside of God's paradise. Hard work, pain, and enmity plagued our kind, but God was already preparing the way of redemption. Through the centuries, the Lord of life oversaw an intricate story. When the time had fully come, God sent his Son to offer us divine adoption. Jesus Christ, the Word made flesh, pitched his tent on our turf. Since we have flesh and blood, he shared in our humanity.

Jesus gave himself in service to others. He touched outcasts. He talked to rejects. He healed the sick. He washed feet. God incarnate spoke divine words. Jesus gave himself in sacrifice to others.

Taking the sin of the world on himself, he suffered at the hands of evil men. He died on their cross and lay in their grave. On the third day, he returned to life, proclaiming victory over death. By his death he freed us who were held in slavery by our fear of death (Heb. 2:14).

Because of our sin, we were God's enemies. Even so he showed his love for us by sending Christ to die for us. He invited us to share in a new way of life. He made possible membership in his family. God called us to join his household, the church of the living God (1 Tim. 3:15).

Working Together in the Church

Those of us who are in Christ are new creatures, but the world still tempts and taunts us to follow its path toward destruction. Individually and corporately, we must commit ourselves to a righteous alternative lifestyle. We must be holy, as God is holy. We must live our lives as strangers here in reverent fear (1 Pet. 1:13-25).

We need other believers in our lives so that we can bless them and so that they can bless us. God does not call us to be Lone Ranger Christians. We do not have complete unity of understanding or practice, but we should at least recognize our unity of purpose. We need to guard the oneness we already share (Eph. 4:3) and work together toward fuller unity (Eph. 4:13).

God's people have had over nineteen hundred years to learn and stretch and grow, but we have frequently made things worse. Rather than devoting ourselves to the apostles' teaching, which came directly from Christ, we have devoted ourselves to various ideologies, letting a host of "issues" break up the fellowship we should share.

We have intentionally divided into many different groups under many different names. This has been a problem since early in church history (1 Cor. 1:10-17), but that does not make it acceptable. We generally use labels to make ourselves feel better and to make other people feel worse. If I am a "_____ Christian," and you are not, then I must be better than you are!

Instead of being "_____ Christians," who exclude others with creeds and confessions, we should be disciples of the Lord Jesus who simply follow the message given to us in the Bible. Accepting another person as a fellow disciple does not imply endorsement of all of his beliefs and opinions. If it did, then none of us could accept anyone else, because we all disagree on some points. Who am I to judge someone else's servant? To his own master he stands or falls (Rom. 14:4).

Most of the Bible is easy to understand. Application often is difficult, but comprehension often is not. Some things are hard to understand, however (2 Pet. 3:16), and earnest disciples have frequently arrived at seemingly contradictory interpretations.

Many of these matters of theological dispute are like coins. They have two sides. No matter how hard you try, you cannot get a good look at both sides of a coin at the same time. Even if you use a mirror, one side will be reversed. You can only accurately study one side at a time.

If you and I were facing each other, and I held a coin up between us, then I could describe one side and you could describe the other. I could insist that my description was correct, and you could insist that your description was correct, and we would both be right!

We tend to approach theological questions with this same sort of limited perspective. At any given time, we can only get a mental handle on one side or the other. We do not have to feel threatened when someone holds a point of view different from the one we hold. If two people can honestly demonstrate Biblical support for their positions, then their seemingly conflicting views may be two sides of the same coin.

We must lay aside our jealousy and strife. Servants of the Lord should not waste time in senseless quarrels, especially with each other (2 Tim. 2:24)! We should pursue those things which lead to peace and edification (Rom. 14:19). We have more in common than we realize.

Only those who desire unity will seek it. Some people seem intent on being heretical, which means divisive in the New Testament. Paul told Titus that after warning such people twice, he need not have anything to do with them (Tit. 3.9-11).

If we are so hung up about our pet doctrines that we cannot enjoy fellowship with anyone else, then we have a serious problem. We may feel that no one nearby is "like us" in their attempt to follow God faithfully. If that is actually the case, then we should humbly invite others to imitate us as we imitate Christ (1 Cor. 11:1). We should be leaders and not wait to be followers.

With those who desire unity, we must ask questions and be willing to give answers. The struggle for mutual understanding and unified action is just that — a struggle. We will wrestle with ourselves, with each other, and with God, but the pursuit of unity is worth the effort.

Besides segregating ourselves from other believers, we have set up religious institutions that impede our spiritual growth. Our emphasis on buildings and programs contrasts sharply with the simplicity displayed by early disciples. Our customs and structures have evolved into seemingly unchangeable patterns. These traditions of men stifle creativity and even cause harm to those involved.

The early believers focused on the apostles' teaching, fellowship, the breaking of bread, and prayer. Their lives were full of wonders and signs, the sharing of possessions, meetings in the temple, fellowship in homes, and praising God. And their numbers kept growing (Acts 2:42-47).

Seeking first God's kingdom is not just a matter of personal piety, nor is it just a matter of church practice. Each generation has work to do in the all-encompassing work of reformation and restoration. Together let us focus on the most important things.

Sharing Good News

People in the world need Jesus whether they realize it or not. They may feel lonely. They may feel burdened. They may feel inadequate. They have good reason to feel this way, for without the Lord, everyone is lonely, burdened, and inadequate.

I grew up in a faithful home. I made my public profession of faith and was baptized at age 13, but that did not stop the tug of the world on my heart. I have relied on my own strength instead of the Lord's. I have been afraid to speak up for him. I have been selfish and foolish and careless. Without divine assistance, I would have been in the same position as those who are without hope and without God in the world (Eph. 2:12).

Thanks be to God through Jesus Christ, who offers us justification and sanctification! By God's power, we can transform our way of thinking. We can destroy our idols and offer ourselves as living sacrifices to the one, true God. His grace allows unbelievers like us to become believers, followers of the Way.

I struggle with knowing when and how to share the good news of Jesus. Fear distracts me – fear of being rejected, fear of turning someone further away, fear of saying the wrong thing. I am not proud of this. What I want to do, I do not do, and what I do, I do not want to do. Those gifted as evangelists deserve our encouragement and support. Those of us gifted in other ways need to use our gifts also in sharing good news. All of us have the power of example and of service.

If I wish to be an effective ambassador for the Lord, then I must act like one. When I fail to live up to my profession of faith, I contribute to God's name being blasphemed (Rom. 2:24). Paul gave instruction about how God's people were to behave so that God's word would not be dishonored and so that the opponent would not have legitimate accusations against us (Tit. 2:1-8).

If following the Lord makes no difference in the way we live, then those outside the church may well wonder why they should come inside. Since skeptics would like to find reasons not to submit to God, we should not give them any additional excuses.

The world has a terrible shortage of well-trained children. This shortage is why we have so many problems in the world. Poorly-trained children grow up to be irresponsible adults who cause problems (and who do not train their children well). I want to counteract this trend by training my children well.

A faithful family can do good together. They can be productive members of their community. They can provide a place of hope and healing. They can show the world what is possible with God. When my children grow up and start households of their own, they can continue and expand the influence.

Giving to the poor and looking after others in need are tangible demonstrations of the love God wants us to share. God commands benevolence. Like all of his commands, this one is a blessing rather than a burden. When we give, we receive.

Genuine generosity opens doors that philosophical precision cannot. If we speak the truth without love, our cymbal clanging will not draw the right kind of attention. If our faith is not illustrated by our deeds, then we are missing the point of faith. Since God is love, we show the world whom we serve when we show love (John 13:35).

We must also be ever ready to give an answer for the hope we have (1 Pet. 3:15). As we become more familiar with Scripture, we will be better able to apply it in all sorts of situations. Scriptural knowledge prepares us to answer a fool in the appropriate way (Prov. 26:4-5). It prepares us to teach, reprove, correct, and train (1 Tim. 3:16-17).

An emotional appeal for a quick prayer of penitence is not the Biblical example of evangelism. Seekers need to know what they are getting into when they acknowledge Jesus as Lord and Christ. They need to count the cost (Luke 14:26-33). They need to change their way of thinking (i.e., repent; Acts 17:30). They need to place their trust in Jesus (Acts 16:31). They need to be buried with Christ through baptism into death (Rom. 6:3-4). As they begin to walk in newness of life, they need to become part of a fellowship of believers who can help them grow (Eph. 4:11-16).

As different members of the body of Christ, we have different gifts. Each of us has an important place to fill in the household of God. We have the opportunity to represent our Father well, to promote the welfare of his family, and to welcome others into it. Make it your ambition to do your part.

Author's Note

Public speakers and writers can come across as if they know everything. Let me tell you a secret: We do not! We are fellow travelers on the same road. I welcome your feedback about this book. Your perspective can help me to improve mine.

Together as God's people, let us move forward in building strong families and strong communities of faith that give a good testimony to the world. By the grace of God, we can lead the way in promoting a multi-generational vision of faithfulness — living for the Lord today and passing on his message to our children and our children's children.

Sharing With Your Group

I am available to speak at homeschool conventions, churches, and other venues about the topics addressed in this book. I can also present a selection of spiritual songs and give portrayals of historic individuals such as Sam Watkins, a Confederate private during the War Between the States; and my grandfather, Wesley Biddle Notgrass, who was an Army sergeant during World War II.

For booking contact:
John Notgrass
370 S. Lowe Ave., Ste A
PMB 211
Cookeville, TN 38501
john@notgrass.com
1-800-211-8793
www.notgrass.com

Resources by John Notgrass Available from The Notgrass Company

Make It Your Ambition **Book**..............................$12.00

My Father's God **CD**..$10.00

> *Eleven songs that praise God, honor family, and encourage faithful living.*

Seasons **CD**...$10.00

> *Twelve songs that explore the blessings and struggles we face during the seasons of our lives.*

"Home Education Past High School"
Audio Cassette...$6.00

> *Thoughts on the benefits of living at home after high school.*

One Soldier's Story **Audio Cassette**....................$6.00

One Soldier's Story **Audio CD**............................$8.00

> *Wesley Biddle Notgrass, John's grandfather, served four years, one month, and seven days in the U.S. Army Medical Corps in New York, England, and Europe from 1941-1945. John offers a first-person portrayal of his experiences.*

Ordering Information

You may order additional copies of this book, music CDs, and audio recordings from the Notgrass Company. We have also written and published world history and American history curricula for high school, Tennessee and Georgia state history curricula for middle school, an art and Bible study series for all ages, a homeschool record-keeping book, drawing instruction, a library skills curriculum, and other unit studies.

To place an order, visit our website, call toll-free, or complete the order form on the other side of this page and mail it to us with your check or money order.

370 S. Lowe Ave., Ste. A
PMB 211
Cookeville, TN 38501

1-800-211-8793

www.notgrass.com

Name	
Address	
Phone	
E-mail	

☐ Add me to your business e-mail list.

Item	Qty	Price	Total
		Shipping	3.00
Sales Tax (Add to total with shipping. 9.75% in TN, 6.25% in IL, local rate in OH and NC)			
		Total Due